A HANDBOOK OF
SCOTLAND'S
COASTS

A HANDBOOK OF
SCOTLAND'S
COASTS

edited by Fi Martynoga

Saraband

Published by Saraband
Digital World Centre, 1 Lowry Plaza
The Quays, Salford, M50 3UB
and
Suite 202, 98 Woodlands Road
Glasgow, G3 6HB, Scotland
www.saraband.net

Editor: Fi Martynoga   Project editor: Sara Hunt

ISBN: 9781912235865

Printed in Great Britain by
Clays Ltd, Elcograf S.p.A.

MIX
Paper from
responsible sources
FSC® C018072
www.fsc.org

CAUTION*: Coastlines are replete with dangers from tides, currents, rocks, cliffs,
erosion, high waves and more, with the risk of being cut off by tides catching out
many people each year. Pollution can be hazardous in some areas. Consuming
wild plants, seaweeds, shellfish and similar items can induce severe (even, in
rare cases, fatal) reactions. Always try new species only with great care and in
very small quantities; check before serving wild plants or seafoods to your guests.
This handbook should **not** be used alone for identification of plant, seaweed or
animal species. Consult the safety guidelines on pages 5–6, 71 and 90, and see
the index for more details, and page 214 for recommended identification guides.*

*Neither the publisher nor the contributors who have compiled this book can
accept any liability for adverse effects incurred during any of the pursuits referred
to in these pages, or by gathering, handling or consuming wild foodstuffs.*

1 2 3 4 5 6 7 8 9 10

The illustrations reproduced in this book are supplied by the contributors, or Saraband Image Library, or else are sourced from shared-resource
and public domain collections, except as noted. Thanks are due to the
following people for colour images shown in the plants, seaweed and
shellfish section (space did not permit credits in situ): Hans Helen Baker,
Cwymhyraeth, Hillavaert, Danielle Langlois, Kruczy, Minghong, Kristian
Peters, Olivier Pichard, Rasbak, Arnstein Ronning, Stemonitis. In the
second colour section, image credits are adjacent to the photographs.

CONTENTS

INTRODUCTION

Picture yourself standing on an island shore at the edge of the Atlantic on a fine spring morning. There is an onshore breeze. Face south and watch the sun catch each curled wave as it makes its way up the shelving beach. It spills thrilling jade green light. It delights, but also makes the watcher melancholy with its inexorable rhythms. In a liminal place, the emotions are in a liminal state, caught between land and water, joy and sadness, 'being' – as Michael Kerrigan puts it in his chapter on coastal culture – 'at the edge of things'.

I have always sought the sea to free up feelings. My guess is that many people do the same. Walking a flat strandline, following the slide of the waves up the sand, and dodging the sudden rush of a stronger reach can work magic on the psyche. To be exposed to the crash of the sea against the rocks of a wild Scottish coast is even more powerful. Even gazing on a flat calm horizon with a view of islands has power to delight at some deep level. (Perhaps this prompted Visit Scotland's 2020 celebration of a Year of Scotland's Coasts and Waters.) Take as an example that extraordinary moment on Skye when you round a headland somewhere near Struan on the Sligachan to Dunvegan road and see below you a view of silver sea, with headlands, islands, and skerries, stretching right across Loch Bracadale to MacLeod's Maidens. That's if you catch the right weather conditions, of course, in that notoriously misty place.

Introduction

Most of us love the seaside. Scotland's wildly indented coast abounds in possibilities. There are rocks and sea stacks where waves leap and foam, or shores where every wave-turned stone is an object of delight. There are quiet inlets, tawny-orange with kelp, picture-perfect coves, and beaches of ground white shell or crumbled black rock. This book is intended to feed your natural delight in getting to the coast. It is a sharing of enthusiasm for places to explore and things you might do once you leave your car or bike and get right down to the shore.

The chapters in this book are written by people who really know and love their subjects. In the course of a career as a writer about hill walking, Ronald Turnbull has built up great expertise in revealing the secrets of geology to a non-expert readership. He's witty, given to anecdotes and has a great turn of phrase: 'Did it crystallise out of Noah's Flood like sugar crystals in the year before last's marmalade?' he asks. And: 'Wrinkles and wiggles of squeezed-out lava decorate the coastline of Fife.' Such informal language makes much more memorable those facts we might all like to have at our fingertips, like the ages of the rocks beneath our feet, and how they got to be where they appear.

As a child, I spent hours rambling along the tideline talking with my father, picking up stones and flotsam, and looking at the remains of 2,000-year-old submerged forests. We would sit using penknives to carve pieces of driftwood into animals and birds. My mother, meanwhile, dozed and read. I always knew we had the better deal, and to this day, I can't sunbathe or just sit at the seaside, though Jim Crumley might teach me how to be still. 'The beachcombing was already three hours old and had stretched into a late lunch, and the tide came in and turned and started to drift back the way it had come, and nothing had stirred that looked remotely otterish.' In the chapter on coastal wildlife from this leading Scottish author, read about the thrilling rewards of being quiet and patiently watching well beyond the moment when most of us would go home. What he observes will astound you.

Michael Kerrigan combines a thorough knowledge of Scotland with scholarship and a great skill with words to take us on a marvellously eclectic tour of our coastal culture. He is great on the 'imaginative excitement we experience at any of the extremities of the Scottish coast – from Cape Wrath or John o'Groats to the Mull of Galloway or Kintyre.' He looks in on art, literature, architecture and music, but goes into more depth about folklore, fishing and seafaring. He makes the observation that the sea used to be the highway. 'The North Channel was far less formidable a barrier than the rugged interiors on either side. The result was that it served as a sort of central plaza around which a disparate assemblage of land territories were grouped, turning our present-day perceptions inside out.' Here he is talking about the sea between Ireland and the west coast of Scotland in the time of our Celtic forbears, but it was true – and not just in that place – until perhaps just two hundred years ago. To see the ports as the hostelries around the edge of a square is to hold a world view very different from the one that prevails today.

Ian Stephen still has that view from the seas, however. He writes as one at the helm, seeing the Scottish coast from a boat. As a sailor and a former coastguard, he really knows his islands and their lore. Eloquent about Scottish maritime history, lighthouses, fishing and coastal trade, he's also a great raconteur with a memory for anecdotes. They vary from the grim 'story of the massacre of the entire population of Eigg in a wide cave with a narrow mouth' to the amusing: 'Ulva is another farming island. Its pastures used to host an unlikely herd of Jersey cows because the current owner liked cream on her strawberries.' He records it all with a fine turn of descriptive phrase – 'the waves are hypnotic, shag-green to male mallard green' – as well.

My own chapters stem from a lifelong interest in the seashore and its flora and fauna. I am not a botanist but an enthusiast for plants, writing for others who might like to know what they are looking at. The details have been checked by professionals, to make sure my amateur enthusiasm didn't run away with itself.

An ancient standing stone on the Isle of Lewis.

Foraging for the delicious little brown shrimps that inhabit the shallowest water on sandy eastern beaches gave me a first glimpse of the bounty that the coastline affords. It was a habitat critical to the survival of our nomadic forebears. They could harvest rock pools in any season, collect seaweed in almost any month, and catch fish whenever tide and weather permitted. We can still do these things, and the chapter on coastal bounty suggests how you can explore the possibilities of seaweeds, shellfish and wild plants safely and sustainably.

How many people understand tides? Sailors are obliged to, but only a dwindling number of ordinary seaside visitors can get their heads around the shifting pattern, or the difference between springs and neaps. Most of us have no more than a notion that tides have something to do with the gravitational pull of the moon and the sun. Spring tides, when the lowest and highest waterlines occur, happen at full and new moons. At these times, the sun is exercising its pull in unison with the moon. Neap tides occur when the moon is in its first, or else its last, quarter, when the sun is pulling in opposition to it. The tidal rise and fall will consequently be much lower than during the spring tides.

Spring tides take around 12 hours 19 minutes to complete a cycle of rising and falling. Neaps take longer, around 12 hours 33 minutes. The whole matter of high and low water is complicated by local phenomena such as currents and winds, which can make the actual behaviour of the sea different from what is published in tide tables. Sudden ebbing (flowing out) can strand small boats, and sudden flowing over shallow beaches like Aberlady (or into the mouths of rocky coves) can take foolhardy walkers completely unawares. We all know the stories, but it is essential to listen to local advice and act with caution in areas known to be perilous. This will become increasingly important as sea levels rise, as they inevitably will when the Greenland ice cap melts in our rapidly heating climate.

Of course, those who take to the sea for recreation, for sea kayaking, surfing, coastal rowing or even cliff scrambling, are usually very well aware of tides. If you have ever felt moved to investigate one of these sports, read the brief accounts that have been contributed by people who are already skilled in (and thrilled by!) one or other of them. In their different ways they all offer glimpses of uniquely vivid ways of experiencing Scotland's coasts.

In the hope that some of our themes may move you enough to seek new horizons along our shores, we have put together a set of descriptions of how you might happily pass time in any of two dozen special places around the mainland coast. From the wonderfully unexplored cliffs of Berwickshire right round to Kirkcudbright, by way of Thurso, Durness and Plockton, our Great Days Out chapter suggests hundreds of interesting ways to spend time at the coast, to see the wildflowers, the rocks or the ruins. We give public transport options and talk about the walking and cycling possibilities for all of them. Please use these where possible, for carbon-emitting car travel must be reduced for the sake of the future of our world. What we have here is so lovely, so varied, wild, and at times so tranquil that it is hard to surpass anywhere in the world. Let's keep it that way.

If you *are* touring by car, Visit Scotland has encouraged people to take a route known as the North Coast 500, from Inverness, west to Applecross, then north via Torridon and Ullapool to the far northwest, then turning east along the north coast. You will see magnificent scenery, remarkable geology, lovely shores and some pleasing settlements. But beware, the NC500 is extremely busy in summer. Expect to dawdle along single-track roads with passing places (always scan ahead and take the nearest one on your left; never cross to a passing place on the other side). It is so popular that you may find the campsites and cafés along the route full. The route is both boon and blessing for the locals, who like the trade but are frustrated by strings of camper vans and sometimes reckless drivers. Please travel the NC500 with consideration for both the land and the locals.

Fi Martynoga

OUR COASTLINES: Who owns the land?

The "coastline" of Scotland is two coastlines; the Mean High Water Springs (MHWS) and the Mean Low Water Springs (MLWS). Between these is the foreshore, the area regularly covered by the tides. Ownership of the foreshore has a fascinating history and remains at the centre of political debate.

To begin with, in the Northern Isles, the foreshore forms part of the land held by the owner of the adjacent land and belongs to the owner of that land. This is a legacy of Norse udal law. Historically, in the rest of Scotland, the foreshore was regarded as the property of the Crown, although the theoretical basis for this claim has changed over the centuries. Originally, it was considered a consequence of sovereignty and of the position of the Crown at the apex of the feudal system of land tenure. Today, however, the accepted legal theory is that it is owned outright by the Crown. Importantly, however, in addition to being the owner of the land, the Crown also acts as guardian of important public rights of navigation, access, fishing and recreation.

During the 19th century, the foreshore was the subject of much litigation. Landowners profited from the kelp industry and were keen to defend what they saw as their proprietorial rights. The Crown was increasingly keen to assert what it believed to be its rights and found itself in conflict with landowners such as the Duke of Argyll who had formed the Association of Seaboard Proprietors. A series of legal disputes sought to resolve the question of who owned the foreshore. It was eventually established that it did indeed belong to the Crown, but not before a number of landowners had successfully acquired title by long periods of possession. Between 1866 and 1945 almost half of the Scottish foreshore had been lost by the Crown on the basis of claims founded on possession, largely through the collection of seaweed by crofters and cottars.

At the time of the first edition of this book (2015), around 50% of the foreshore outwith the Northern Isles remained in the ownership of the Crown and formed part of the Crown Estate in Scotland, administered and managed by the Crown Estate Commissioners under the Crown Estate Act 1961. For over twenty years, there had been calls for the Crown Estate to be made more accountable. Since devolution in 1999, the independence referendum of 2014 and the constitutional debates that followed, there were growing demands for devolution of control over the foreshore and other Crown property rights.

A series of Parliamentary inquiries recommended reform. The Scottish Crown Estate Act 2019 transferred some responsibilities for managing the foreshore and seabed to local organisations, initially on a pilot basis.

At the time of this updated edition (spring 2020), new questions on the future of our coastal communities have arisen following the Brexit referendum, but long-awaited change to foreshore and seabed ownership and management has begun.

Andy Wightman MSP

(Updated 2020 by the editors)

ONE

THE GEOLOGY OF OUR SEASHORE

I must begin with these stones as the world began
Hugh MacDiarmid 'On a Raised Beach', 1934

"Scotland small?" asks Hugh MacDiarmid – the words are carved in beach granite from Caithness in the wall of the Scottish Parliament. And his poem of 1974 describes the variety of life in one small patch of heather. How much less small, then, when you take the whole of Scotland's coastline: 6,718km, according to the Ordnance Survey, for the mainland alone, and three times that if you add in all the islands.

From the shell beaches of the Hebrides to the twisted grey cliffs of Galloway and the red seastacks of Dunbar, from the mudflats and saltmarsh of the Solway to the basalt caves of Mull, Scotland has almost every kind of coastal formation there is; from almost every age of the earth, halfway back to when the planet cooled enough to congeal into continents. And with the wandering of those continents, Scotland's cliffs and boulders come from the southern oceans, and unknown places even earlier.

The Geology of our Seashore

Understanding of it starts at a scrap of sea cliff called Siccar Point, just south of Cove Harbour on the Berwickshire coast. In 1788, at the full flowering of the Edinburgh Enlightenment, James Hutton and John Playfair came ashore here from a small boat. And what they saw, embedded in the coastline of today, was a scrap of coastline from 360 million years ago.

The rock here is the harsh, layered greywacke – a dark, grainy type of sandstone – of the Southern Uplands, tilted up on edge by some cataclysm (by, we now know, the collision of Scotland and England in the Ordovician period). A few yards out to sea, the seaworn slabs form small upright walls, ready to tear out the bottom of their boat if they'd been careless with the oars. A few yards up from the tideline, just the same small walls, but half-buried in red sandstone.

Scotland small?

There is no correct figure for the length of Scotland's coastline, as this depends on the length of your ruler.

The OS figure is measured digitally from a map at 1:10,000 scale. A smaller scale map gives a shorter coastline, as it skips many of the wiggles.

Mathematically, the 'fractal dimension' of Scotland's coast is 1.25, meaning that if you increase the map scale by a factor of 10, you increase the measured length by 75%.

If you measured the coastline on the ground itself, in theory you'd get a figure of about 70,000km, nearly twice the circumference of the Earth. And through a low powered microscope, going around the bumps in every grain of sand, it'd be about 1 million km!

'Scotland in miniature'

Arran's tourist-board slogan is correct; the small island does cram together scenery gathered from all over the country. The Highland Line itself passes right across the island: the south of the island is Central Lowlands, while north of the String road is true Highlands. There lies the single sea loch – but Loch Ranza's a good one, complete with ruined castle on its island.

In the west the single road (two lanes, but only just) runs along the flat grass of the raised beach that carries it around much of the island. The landscape is borrowed from west Ayrshire; but the emptiness, and the clean Atlantic air, give it an atmosphere that belongs well north of the Highland line. The back of the former beach has former sea-caves, carved into the Old Red Sandstone. King Robert the Bruce sheltered here in 1307, and was encouraged by a spider to keep on getting defeated by the English. (Or perhaps not: there are at least two other 'Bruce's Caves' in southern Scotland and the spider itself was first recorded, or even invented, by Walter Scott.)

In the south are more cliffs of red sandstone – the New Red Sandstone, this time, rather less common in Scotland than the Old Red is. The cliffs are quite low, and flat-topped, and on the seawashed boulders the seals play tummy-bounce to keep an eye on the walker passing by.

The eastern seafront has the palm trees and faded pavilions of Glasgow's Clyde playground. Scotland in miniature? There's even a scaled-down St Andrews: the crazy golf along Brodick's esplanade.

Those small walls were carved by some much earlier sea: a sea that had risen, and dropped its sand around them, layer upon layer all up the cliffs above. In the bottom layer of that red sand are sea-smoothed pebbles, the beach shingle of that long-ago shoreline.

But what of the tilted greywacke layers underneath? Before whatever force had raised them on edge, they too had fallen, grain by grain, layer on layer, upon the floor of some even earlier ocean. And the grains of sand that formed the greywacke: from what even earlier content had they been washed out by rain and wind of what even more distant age? John Playfair's mind "seemed to grow giddy by looking so far into the abyss of time.

Scotland? No, not small at all. The rock platform at Siccar Point – just big enough for a BBC crew filming 'Men of Rock' last time I stood on it – is a three-minute trailer for an epic movie 2 billion years long. The tilted greywacke is the ocean floor that once lay between Scotland and England. When the two countries collided, about 450 million years ago, this sea-bed sludge was raised into the open air, tilted over, and crumpled like a used paper hanky. Those grey rocks lie within what we now call the Southern Uplands, emerging as sea cliffs at Mull of Galloway and Fast Castle. The Old Red Sandstone on top – by Scottish standards quite a young sandstone – is desert dunes and flash flood gravel, rubble eroded out from the great Caledonian mountain chain. Those mountains, Himalaya-high, rose as the two bits of continent crunched together. Their worn-away roots now make the Scottish Highlands.

Scotland's Central Lowlands: the coal hole

Over the past thousand years, the Fife coast has been a busy place. Small boats have traded between Fife's farmland and Edinburgh, carrying corn and kale, fish and the salt to preserve it in. Every bay has its little sea-port, the houses and harbour walls of orange-brown sandstone.

Raised beaches

Fife's seastacks stand not on the shingle but in cow-pasture, several metres up from the shoreline. They were shaped by an earlier sea, one when the land was lower than today.

Since the ice melted off the top, Scotland has been rising – and still is, at several millimetres a year. At many places around Scotland's coastline, at the back of today's beach there's a level area which, if you dig into it, is beach shingle. At its back will be a former sea cliff.

Fife's Maiden Rock and Caiplie Caves were shaped by a sea of about 5,000 years ago, some 5m higher than today. And many of Fife's sea caves are now high and dry above the current tideline, conveniently placed for saints, kings and brigands. Constantine I, last Pictish King of Scotland, sheltered in one near Crail and was killed in it after the battle against the Vikings in AD874. It was in a cave at East Wemyss that King James III, wandering incognito as the Gaberlunzie Man, dropped in on some brigands. The raised-beach cave of Sawney Bean, the cannibal, is on the Ayrshire coast just north of Ballantrae.

Geologically, too, there's a lot going on. The limestone bands are lumpy with ancient crinoids (sea lilies) and coral. The red-brown sandstones are speckled with seashells. Scavenging shrimps and fierce predatory worms have burrowed through them. And the warm browns are streaked through with black: twigs and tree-roots, and narrow layers of coal plucked away by the sea. On the foreshore at Crail is a fossil tree stump, wide enough to spread a picnic on. A few metres away are footprints of a monster millipede, 2m long, that strode across those tropical sands.

The coal is a clue here. These rocks are from the Carboniferous period: the time when the UK was drifting northwards across the Equator, a stinky swamp of giant ferns, giant frogs, and dragonflies the size of seagulls.

Arthur's Seat

Geologists refer to the Lowlands as Scotland's 'Midland Valley'. It is in fact a rift valley, formed when Scotland was being stretched north–south during the breakup of the Pangaea supercontinent. Between the Highland Boundary fault (the 'Highland Line'), and the equally well marked Southern Upland fault line, this middle bit of Scotland has simply sunk. And so these younger rocks lie alongside the ancient Southern Upland greywackes, and the very, very ancient schists of the Highlands.

Formed as it is between two fault-line cracks down through the Earth's crust, a rift valley features volcanoes. Alongside Africa's Great Rift Valley lies Kilimanjaro. Long-crumbled volcanoes of central Scotland have left their central lava-plugs as Arthur's Seat *(shown above)* and the Bass Rock island. Wrinkles and wiggles of squeezed-out lava decorate the coastline of Fife. Basalt dykes run into the sea, black and shiny between the sea-washed sandstone. Flat dolerite sills form the flat-topped Isle of May. Tough volcanic rocks gave the monks of Inchcolm their sea-resistant but harshly infertile island refuge.

Look away northwards or south for ancient rocks, high cliffs and romantic grandeur. From the broken towers of St Andrews Cathedral, down to the abandoned pithead gantries of Kircaldy, the Fife coast is intimate and wiggly. Even the cheerful orange pantiles are determined by geology. Elsewhere, Scotland's slates are formed by compression: the great earth movements of the

Scotland–England collision. Fife's rocks are too young for that, and unsquashed. But Fife's coalfields are fire kilns for baking clay into tiles. That coal also fuelled the salt industry, the steam rising from boiling seawater all along this shore.

Alternating with the stone towers that defend this strategic sea-coast, a set of whimsical seastacks worthy of Spanish architect Antoni Gaudi. Maiden Rock, like a crumpled cardboard box left out in the rain. Buddo Rock, wrinkled and pink, slashed in half as if by the Devil's tail. Caiplie Caves, with sea mist off the Forth drifting through the empty arches. And for contrast, there's one in black basalt. The Rock & Spindle is part of the internal plumbing of a small volcano. The 'spindle' on its side is a whirl of basalt columns, collapsed outwards. The 'rock' is slender and tilted, 12m high. My grandfather, a mathematician and climber, left a silver sixpence on its top for the next visitor; but found it still up there a few years later.

Old Man, old sand

Orkney is a different place altogether – for the Orcadians, 'Scotland' means all the other parts of Scotland not including Orkney. After the antique and mangled rocks of the Highlands, Orkney is a well-behaved landscape that could be the meadows of Herefordshire. Except that 80% of it's not there: taken away by the sea. The air is free of the pollution us southerners long ago stopped noticing like the dirt on our spectacles – and the unworldly light is doubled by the reflection of the sea that's just behind the low curve of the hill.

Timber here is a luxury, and fence wire is twisted between upright slabs of gritty red sandstone. Stone Age man built those flat slabs into doorsteps and kitchen cabinets at Scara Brae. They stand high in the cherry-red cathedral of St Magnus at Kirkwall, and higher still in the tottering, crumbly-cornered Old Man of Hoy *(opposite)*. Below the slabby cliffs, the ever-anxious sea washes against oval stones striped pink and ochre like beach balls, if the beach balls were in faded sepia photos of long ago.

The Geology of our Seashore

The Old Man of Hoy

Just round the corner from Stromness, I walked to another fragment of ancient shoreline. Back in the Devonian period, 'Stromness' was a granite island, rising from an inland sea filling up with red sand. Granite beach-back rock of 400 million years ago has once again become a beach-rock of today. Around its base lie seawashed pebbles of granite and red sandstone. Scraping away the shingle, the same stones of granite, sea-smoothed by the ancient waves of Lake Orkadie, are now embedded in red sandstone rock.

This Old Red Sandstone lies immediately below the Carboniferous with its coal, sandstone and limestone; comes from the period immediately before, the Devonian. At that time 'Scotland' was south of the Equator, moving northwards through the zone that's now the deserts of Namibia. Through Scotland's Lowlands, the Old Red Sandstone emerges from below the Carboniferous as red desert sand-dunes, or red pebbly layers from flash floods and mountain wadis. It makes red-brown sea cliffs at Dunbar, Largs and Arbroath. Grim Dunnottar Castle, at Stonehaven, stands on layer on layer the colour of dried blood, with rounded pebbles like the skulls of dead fighters.

But from Cromarty to a corner of Norway, the red sand drifted into an enclosed inland lake, Scapa Flow but thirty times as wide. In Lake Orkadie's clear waters swam weird armoured fish, ancestors not just of subsequent fish but also of anything with bones inside it, four-legged life on land, and us. In the stagnant depths lived nothing at all, and a fish that fell down there was preserved in black mud for ever. Or at least until the early 19th century, when Hugh Miller from Cromarty, side-whiskered stonemason and passionate Protestant, cracked open the stones.

In a story by Jorge Luis Borges, he meets an old man who sells him 'The Book of Sand', so called because you never see the same page twice, and neither the book nor the sand has any beginning or any end. The bookseller isn't named, but is from the Orkneys – an Old Red Sandstone man.

Ocean-bottom sludge

From James Hutton's Siccar Point *(below)*, turn south along the Berwickshire coast. Behind you are turnip fields, their mud the warm brown of the Old Red Sandstone. But ahead the clifftops rise in whin and bracken. The cliffs themselves are dreary sandstone, the colour of a winter afternoon; grey gritty slabs piled for miles ahead, to where the matching ruin of Fast Castle pokes into the fading sky.

This is the greywacke, and it stretches across Scotland to Ayrshire and the Mull of Galloway. Dreich as they are when the

Siccar Point

light fades on a drizzly day, they started life yet more deep and dreary: sea-bottom mud in the trenches of a vanished ocean. That ocean – we call it Iapetus – gradually shrank between two advancing continents. The underwater sludge was squashed up between like treading on a tube of toothpaste.

At Sandyhills, the Solway mudflats stretch towards distant England, with the scratchy, zigzag line of a salmon haaf-net (a net design brought to us by the Vikings) and the distant dots of the Robin Rigg Wind Farm. Straight out of the slurry the greywacke rises, dark slabs bent and tipped on end, and a sea arch that soars above a pool of mud. For those whose patriotism is igneous and geological, there's visible resentment here that Scotland has been so mangled by its southern neighbour.

Down on the foreshore, the sea has picked at the grey slabs like a busy gossip, exposing their long-ago story. Dirt drifts out to sea, builds up on the edge of the continental shelf. An earth-quake, or just the ten-millionth speck of grit, sends the whole pile over the edge. A turbulent mix of water and powdered stone tumbles out across the sea bed at 50 miles per hour, snapping submarine cables as it goes. Each of the grey slabs, 10cm or a metre in thickness, is one of these underwater avalanches, the rock layer laid in a minute or so as it comes to rest. Its top surface can preserve ripples. They look like the ripples left in the Solway sand as the tide goes out; but are the last water current that flowed along the top of the avalanche as its energy died, kilometres down in the deep ocean.

Meanwhile the bottom surface of the slab has lumps and bulges called slump structures, where heavy sludge flopped into the softer sea bed. And in between the slabs is fine mudstone, hollowed out between the sea. While each slab is 60 seconds of sludge-pile arrival, the thin layer between them is thousands of years of nothing-happening before and after.

Over at Mull of Galloway, or across in Berwickshire, that's it. The greywacke's simple story: seafloor avalanche slabs, lifted and crumpled by the Scotland–England collision. Here at

Sandyhills, it gets more interesting. Pinkish streaks of crystalline rock wiggle through the Needle's Eye arch. James Hutton looked up at these with particular interest. Over at Siccar Point it was sandstone lying on top of sandstone, both sorts made from washed-away remains of even earlier sorts of stone. This all has to start somewhere. The big blob of the nearby Criffel granite, grey and speckly, and formed from mineral crystals rather than sand, is an example of that 'somewhere'. Was it created by God brand new on Day 3 (Tuesday 25th October 4004BC)? Did it crystallise out of Noah's Flood like sugar crystals in the year before last's marmalade? The pinkish streaks at Needle's Eye are the extreme edge of the granite, and they aren't either original or an evaporite. They've squeezed in, red hot and melted, through the cracks in the dark slabby greywacke.

After passing through this arch of Enlightenment, perhaps more clear-headed than before but certainly with much muddier feet, another mile gets you confused all over again. The cliffs above are tilted-up greywacke, as before. But the foreshore is brownish sandstone, lying roughly flat, eroded in honeycomb hollows by the salt water. Just like the Midland Valley, the Solway Firth is a former rift valley. The northern fault line follows the Scotland shore. Along much of that Galloway coastline there's a narrow strip of the younger Carboniferous rocks, resembling the ones in East Lothian and Fife. The greywacke does have fossils: the ocean-floating graptolites, so ancient and inscrutable they look like random scratches. But along this strip of Solway, there are proper fossils: plant fragments here at Sandyhills; shells; some really convincing corals at Borran Point southwest of Dumfries.

Think back now to Siccar Point. The Old Red Sandstone on top lay more or less level; this Southern Upland greywacke underneath is the covered-over trauma of the Scotland–England collision. From here on down, like a psychologist delving into the deep unconscious, all rocks will be mangled and bent by the Caledonian mountain-building crunch; and the older ones by even earlier disasters.

Loch Hourn, off the Sound of Sleat, north of the Knoydart Peninsula

The Highlands: schist with a twist

From the end of a very long single-track road, an old path leads on westwards along the shore of Loch Hourn. The loch is salt, fringed with tidal pebbles and seaweed. But ahead, it bends through a gap between two mountains; you can't see the open sea at all.

The path was built for ponies by Victorian deer-stalkers. Where the drainage has broken down, it's soggy black mud. But most of it is stony-surfaced, with a ditch on the uphill side, and stone culverts at each of the descending streams. The ground is heather, and bog myrtle, and yellow spikes of bog asphodel; then the bright green and orange of sphagnum mosses. The path takes a clever line finding the drier places, the rock slabs and the heathery terraces, along the steep side-slope of Sgurr Sgiath Airigh. At 20km in from the Sound of Sleat, sea waves are small or absent. There are no sea cliffs, and no beaches. The hillside slope just hits the shoreline and carries on down underwater. The seaweed mixes its salty scent with the faint honey of the heather that dangles a few feet above.

The gouging effects of glaciation left this distinctive valley shape

Loch Hourn *(previous page)* is not a bay, hollowed out along some softer layer of rock. It's not a flooded estuary like the Firth of Clyde. Loch Hourn is in fact a fjord, 100m deep as it emerges into the Sound of Sleat. Fjords are formed by glaciers. When water in its liquid form reaches the low ground it levels off and loses its landscape power. But a glacier just keeps on downhill, gouging out a trough that can be hundreds of metres deeper than the natural sea bed.

Here to north of the Highland Line, the rocks are the roots of the mountain chain called the Caledonian, which rose to a height of 5,000m or more as the crumple zone of the Scotland–England collision. Those rocks are folded, mangled, and tough; which is why, after half a billion years out in the rain and wind, the sturdy stumps of them still stand at one-fifth of their original height. In the west, especially, those mountain heights attracted snow, piling into ice under its own weight. And the mountain slopes slid the glaciers back westward, gnawing deep slots out towards the sea. The result: this splendidly crinkly coastline, and ice-shaped pointy mountains rising straight up out of the sea.

The mangled rocks are grey and greyish-white, wiggly-patterned from the crumple movements. Badger-striped beach pebbles, and just here and there specks gleaming red across a shoreline rock or polished sea boulder. In Gaelic legend the Sluagh Sidhe, the ghostly airborne army that gathers dead souls, leaves drops of blood as it passes overhead. In geology, equally, the blood-red specks are the sign of violence. These semi-precious garnets form at a particular point of heat and pressure, deep underneath the forming mountain chain.

These grey schist rocks form shoreline from the Clyde north-wards to Lochalsh and the bridge to Skye. The stones are old: 'Precambrian' means before the first of the ten named geological periods, before the start of life with hard shells and fossils, 500 million years ago and earlier.

Roderick Impey Murchison gets it wrong

The old and inaccessible rocks of the north are most easily seen along their edge: the shoreline. In the 1810s, a Mr MacCulloch sailed along the north coast and made some sketches. At John o' Groats was the Old Red Sandstone, its familiar slabby lay-ers standing in the magnificent stacks of Duncansby Head. Westwards just before Cape Wrath was more red sandstone; given a harbour to get ashore at, some free time, and a hammer, it ought to offer some more of Mr Miller's fossil fish. Between the two was the grey, streaky, crystalline schist rock, as seen in the southern Highlands, such as at Loch Hourn with its steamer service from Fort William. Here in the far north the schist was interrupted by beds of limestone, and also by a white, brittle stone they called 'quartz rock' (today's name for it is quartzite). Underneath the red sandstone at Cape Wrath, forming lumpy moorlands right out to the Outer Hebrides, was a greyer and more lumpy sort of the schist.

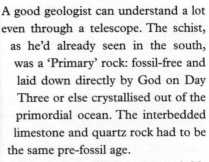

A good geologist can understand a lot even through a telescope. The schist, as he'd already seen in the south, was a 'Primary' rock: fossil-free and laid down directly by God on Day Three or else crystallised out of the primordial ocean. The interbedded limestone and quartz rock had to be the same pre-fossil age.

Unfortunately, Wick coastguard Mr Charles Peach was merely an amateur dabbler. So when his work took him to Durness harbour he went poking around in the limestone looking for fossils. And there they were, even if mostly wormholes rather than seashells or trilobites.

A really good geologist can understand a lot even from hundreds of miles away in Durham. Roderick Impey Murchison was born in Easter Ross and became an officer in Wellington's army fighting the French in Spain. When he didn't have enough cash to devote the rest of his life to hunting and shooting, geology was almost as much fun, and cheaper. He helped sort out the Old Red Sandstone and some same-aged limestone in southern Devon, and thus to 'erect' the Devonian period. He travelled to the Urals in Russia, found fossil rocks corresponding with some of the New Red Sandstone, and erected another period. He called that one the Permian after a Russian town, and the grateful Tsar presented him with a truly magnificent jewelled snuffbox, now on display in the Cromwell Road. But his favourite erection was the Silurian period; fossil-bearing rocks in Shropshire lying immediately under (and before) the Old Red Sandstone.

Already he'd traced his Silurian stones westwards into Wales, and across Scotland's Southern Uplands. And now, in a flash of insight, he identified the Durness wormholes as being from the earliest fossils of all, the Cambrian period. This annexed the whole of northern Scotland, above these limestones and below the red sandstones, into his Silurian empire.

One geologist, Professor Nicol, wasn't as thrilled as he should have been by this radical rewriting of the geology books. He'd been there, and observed that the quartz rock and limestone lay on top of (rather than underneath) the western sandstone. Anyone who's climbed or even looked at Liathach or Beinn Eighe can confirm this. And where the schist was above the limestone and quartzite, the junction was not a simple layering, but involved fault lines and squeezed-in igneous rocks. Nicol was only from Aberdeen, while Murchison was director of the Geological Survey (not to mention erector of those three geological periods). Science cannot abide suppression; but Murchison could arrange for Nicol's wrong notions to be presented on Day Three of the conference after everyone had taken the early train back to London.

What else should Murchison have spotted? However much you hammer the red sandstones of Wester Ross, you won't

The cliffs at Whitten Head, Sutherland

find any fossil fish – or fossil anything. Old as are the Old Red Sandstones, the Torridonian Sandstone (as we now call it) is three times as old again, from long before the start of shelly life.

And there's one of those questions too big and obvious to ask. Back when the squiggly crystalline schist was something formed on a sea bed, it could lie in among the limestone. But once it was understood as metamorphic – squashed and melted up remains of earlier rocks – then yes, there could be younger layers of limestone lying on top. But unsquashed, unsquiggled limestone underneath? The schist and limestone are as they are. Nobody noticed that the 'how come?' question had casually un-answered itself.

It took nearly 50 years to sort it out. The sorters were Ben Peach, son of the coastguard who found the Durness fossils, and his friend and colleague John Horn. They spent 14 years (1883–1897) knocking around the north-west in heavy boots and scruffy old tweeds, Mr Horn being slightly less scruffy than Mr Peach. The schist of central Scotland is indeed older than fossils, and a whole lot older than the Silurian: it's Precambrian, around 1 billion years. The Scotland–England crunch, and the rising of the Caledonian mountain chain, has squeezed this schist out sideways in a surprising way. Chunks of landscape, hundreds of kilometres wide but only a few hundred metres thick, have moved westwards like the leaf of an extendable table. It's called the Moine Thrust. On any geological map of Scotland, it shows as a squiggly line from Durness on the north coast, right down the western edge, running into the sea just south of the Isle of Skye.

What the schist was shoving sideways into was a different country, of even more magnificent mountains. The red Torridonian sandstone rises as Liathach and An Teallach, all topped with the off-white 'Quartz Rock' or Cambrian quartzite. And what these mountains stand on is not at all that ancient eastern schist, but a stone even more squiggly, rough and grey, and much, much older still: the Lewisian Gneiss.

A gneiss wee walk

On the north side of Loch Torridon, any moorland lochan may contain the Beiste, or water-horse, and every fifth rock knoll is named for the Sith, or fairies. The old Postie's Path that runs from Alligin around to Diabaig is in true fairy style: misleading, with a hint of malice. It bends up through a tiny pass, circles one of the hidden lochans, and shows the sea again in a quite unexpected direction. A final grassy saddle sees Diabaig suddenly ahead. But bare, ice-scraped rocks reach down from the moorland, and you must drop to the sea, edge up a ledge, and drop to the sea all over again before scrambling down a tree root to the village edge.

This knock-and-lochan landscape was scraped to its current shape by the edge of the Atlantic ice sheet, at 'breakfast time this morning' in geological time. But the rocks themselves are ancient. This Lewisian Gneiss is a scrap of continental crust that's been knocking about for at least 2 billion years. That's half the age of the Earth and Solar System, and about one-eighth of the Universe itself since the Big Bang.

Glen Torridon

Heat and pressure deep underground have partly recrystallised it. Crystal corners make it rough and grippy, good to clamber about on wherever it's not covered in bogland slime. Black dykes of basalt run through it, broken and illegible like headlines in a crumpled newspaper. The news they carry is mountain building and moving continents in geological ages yet to be retraced. Here and there the gneiss has melted altogether, and pink streaks of granite run down a knoll side into the waves.

This rugged old stuff doesn't form sea cliffs, or break down into beaches. For making sand, the easiest stuff is sandstone. The Torridonian sandstone has been carried on the back of the gneiss for about a billion years, still sitting the right way up and uncrumpled, hardly even tilted sideways. This is pure geological fluke, and it's not so surprising Mr MacCulloch was tricked into mistaking it for the (in this context not old at all) Old Red Sandstone.

It's at Sandwood Bay that the sea gets into the Torridonian, and makes sea cliff and beach. The cliffs run out to a tottery seastack, its lower half hazed with sea spray, standing in dislocated blocks and ledges against the sunset. The beach is a mile and a half wide, backed with marram dunes and pokey lumps of gneiss. The wind sings across the sand grains; the sunset shines pink through the wave breakers.

Streams cut into the sandstone; the clifftops northwards are well drained and grassy underfoot for the half-day walk northwards. Cape Wrath foghorn stands above pinkish Lewisian slabs and blue-green restless sea. The white-harled lighthouse crumbles in the wind; across 20 miles of Pentland Firth, and 2 billion years up in time, the Orkneys raise flat slabs of Old Red Sandstone. A minibus full of birdwatchers clatters down the dirt road and stops between the old sheds.

A raised beach at Whalsay

Chiliad by chiliad
What bricole piled you here, stupendous cairn?

[Chiliad: thousand-year period; bricole: complex rebounding shot in billiards]

No, Scotland is not small. The rocks around our coastline are an exploration that's at least a lifetime long – or, to look at it the other way, extends over a full 2 billion years.

Geologists tell their stories downwards, from the present back into deep time. Re-emerging from the depths up to the ground surface of today, the tale has five chapters. The Lewisian Gneiss, gnarled and ancient continental crust. The schist (Moine and Dalradian), somewhat less ancient, squashed sideways by the Scotland–England collision. The greywacke, deep ocean sludge squeezed upwards from between the two continents by that same collision. The Old Red Sandstone: rubble washed out of those crunched-up mountains, lying roughly level and itself uncrunched. And on top of that, the coral beaches and rain-forest swamps of the Carboniferous period.

But that short summary leaves out so much... Above it all, Scotland does have scraps of the Jurassic, surprising us with ammonites in a corner of Cromarty. And a mere 50 million years ago, right alongside the most ancient gneiss, the opening of the Atlantic has poured out ocean-ridge rocks, so recent you can almost feel the heat on your cheek: the basalt column cave at Staffa, and high black cliffs of Skye.

Smoo Cave in Sutherland is where old and crumpled limestone meets salt water in a bit of Mediterranean landscape. The Outer Hebrides have long western beaches not of sand (gneiss is too tough to crumble down to sand) but of shell, broken by the waves, blowing inland to make fertile machair grassland with wild flowers and the uncanny rattle of the corncrakes. At Ballantrae, the crunch of the continents has shoved up rock from below the deep ocean, from below the earth's crust itself, rock that shudders at the touch of air and degenerates into red and green streaked serpentine.

Shetland is a mash-up of most of Scotland, slotted with glens and sea lochs by the ice sheets moving south. The eastern island, Whalsay, is central-Scotland schist; but a raised beach near Sodom could show pebbles too of Old Red Sandstone, volcanic basalt, and sub-ocean serpentine – all nudged around the islands one wave at a time. And add to them occasional ice-born bits of Norway.

'On a Raised Beach' is one of the great Scottish poems. It piles together tough and ancient words from geology, biology, the classics and even billiards; like a geological text, it's best read online for one-click dictionary access. "Glaucous, hoar, enfouldered, cyathiform": one small beach in the Shetlands contains the universe, and man within it.

Ronald Turnbull

TWO

COASTAL
WILDLIFE

The Laureate of the Scottish coast is surely Gavin Maxwell. He found the high watermark of his writer's muse in a lighthouse keeper's cottage on a West Highland shore where the Atlantic crams into the Sound of Sleat between the mainland and south Skye. The place is called Sandaig, but it travelled the world under the name he gave it, Camusfearna, in the book that made his name. Single-handedly he opened our eyes to the persuasive magic of otters, and of life both wild and human on the edge of the land. In *Ring of Bright Water* he wrote:

> *There is a perpetual mystery and excitement in living on the seashore, which is in part a return to childhood and in part because for all of us the sea's edge remains the edge of the unknown; the child sees the bright shells, the vivid weeds and red sea-anemones of the rock pools with wonder and with the child's eye for minutiae; the adult who retains wonder brings to his gaze some partial knowledge which can but increase it, and he brings, too, the eye of association and of symbolism, so that at the edge of the ocean he stands at the brink of his own unconscious.*

Maxwell's own childhood was on the Galloway coast. Near the place where he grew up there is a beautiful bronze sculpture to his memory – a sculpture not of the man but of an otter.

Otters

My favourite coastal pastime is beachcombing. For otters. I can think of no happier way to fritter away a whole day. Because sometimes it takes a whole day. For example:

The beachcombing was already three hours old and had stretched into a late lunch, and the tide came in and turned and started to drift back the way it had come, and nothing had stirred that looked remotely otterish. I did all the things I do when I am looking for otters and there are none. I watched birds, picked up shells, scribbled in a notebook, drank coffee, and finally decided on lunch. Often, when an otter does eventually turn up on such a day, it does so right in the middle of the very land-and-seascape you have been scrutinising for hours yet you never saw it arrive there. There is a law of nature that dictates such things but I am no nearer to recognising its symptoms now than I was when I first started watching otters more than 45 years ago.

With lunch followed by a long stillness and a wind that blew from sea to shore that suited my purpose, I went back to work, which means sitting still and staring. Finally I found amid the suck and blow of slow, shallow waves beneath the listless, whispering seaweed a furrow that was surely too straight to be the work of a conspiracy of sea and wrack and rock. But it was not an otter. It was two otters, swimming so deliberately nose-to-tail that they were only separable with the help of binoculars.

I was sitting on the low ledge of a small cliff, and ready to move nearer the water's edge as soon as the otters dived, but they did not dive. Instead, the leading otter turned at right angles towards the very shore where I sat. So I froze and the two otters nose-to-tailed straight towards me. The ring-leader otter kept uttering a hoarse, interrogative back-of-the-throat "Haah?" which, I like to think, asks at least three questions: who are you, what are you, and what are you up to?

Both otters reached the shallows and stood up on hind legs with perfectly synchronised choreography (do they practise?).

Then they barked that same question again, twice and in perfect unison. The second otter lost its nerve, or was just bored by the turn of events; it back-flipped and rolled away into deep water and vanished.

But the first otter stood its ground, still stood erect, and said "Haah!" every few seconds. I have met this phenomenon before, and by copying the sound, I have – very occasionally – participated in a protracted conversation several minutes long without having the slightest idea what kind of message I was communicating. Mostly, nature ignores this kind of mimicry, but very occasionally, it lures the creature closer. Stoats and weasels in particular will respond to any kind of whistle or click or kissing noises. It is interesting (or at least it interests me) that stoats and otters are two of the most likely to respond to a human summons, given that they belong to the same wea-sel tribe. Curiosity appears to be a reliable component of their workaday lives.

Then the second otter was back, a fabulously-built, thick-set dog otter swimming and stomping hugely all around what I had already judged to be a bitch. Now he was trying to lure her away from her obsessive interest in this shoreline intruder, which, for all its otter noises, was clearly not an otter. He barrel-rolled in the

water, which seemed to impress me more than it did her, for she turned on him in a lithe and leathery swirl, snapped her jaws close to his muzzle, and at once she was standing again and out of the water now and challenging me with her breathy bark. "Haah!"

Again and again the dog otter lured her into the water, and again and again she toyed with him or snapped at him and returned to stare me out. Then she uncoiled back into the water through wrack and among rock and dived through whirlpools of her own making. In the flowing of the otters and the surge and retreat of water, the restless heave of the seaweed, nature contrived a kind of mesmerism, a mobile jigsaw puzzle in which all the pieces constantly moved yet none was ever out of place, the puzzle never incomplete.

Then she was back. She stood on her hind legs again and now with one foot in the water and one out on the stone shore. She had, it seemed, chosen to include me in whatever fascination was occupying her otter mind. And – again, it seems to me – she had started to turn my mimicry of her voice into a game. Whenever she returned to the shore, she stood and uttered that same sound. If I did not respond at once, she repeated it again and again until I did, at which point she whirled round and dived into the waves again. Then she added a new twist.

She squirmed along a rock ledge just above the sea and vanished where the ledge turned behind the rock. Her tail was the last of her to vanish. Seconds later her head reappeared where her tail had vanished, and with the rest of her body still hidden,

she barked at me again. I responded. She reversed out of sight. Then she inched forward again and peered round the rock. "Haah!" she said again.

I sat motionless, suppressing bubbling up childhood instincts to giggle, and to run and hide myself. Whether or not she became bored by my stillness, or whether she had reached her natural boredom threshold for one thing before she must explore the next, I have no way of knowing. I have often thought since then that I should have tried to hide too, and see if she responded differently, but stillness is what brought her to me in the first place, and I suppose I reasoned at the time that any movement would have ended the thing before it was done. Anyway, she got bored.

She leaped off her rock, and in my mind as I write this is an image of her frozen in mid-air, all four legs splayed wide, her tail straight out, her jaws wide open. And in that attitude she thudded into the water, and two otters rolled away from the chaos.

The next I saw of them they were a hundred yards away, swimming companionably north. I wonder what it is that otters do when they swim off in tandem knowing they have hopelessly beguiled a human bystander. Or perhaps they knew no aftermath and they were already preoccupied with the day's next adventure. Perhaps the only aftermath is mine, the exclusive preserve of one who likes nothing better than to go beachcombing for otters.

A big fish

The Mull of Galloway (see Portpatrick, page 207) is an outpost of an outpost. So many tides and currents jig and reel and bop and boogie beneath its cliffs that ancient mariners used to drag their boats across the low-lying, 200-yards-wide neck of land between East and West Tarbet a mile west of the Mull rather than dice with that reckless collision of seas. On a rare wind-free day with added late spring sun, a cliff-top ledge is a good place from which to try and fathom out the sea's unfathomable, gruff-voiced mayhem. Water moves in every direction, here in a deep and slow swell, there in sharp-crested breaking waves that whiten as they collapse then lapse into a crowd of whirlpools, and on either side of all that the sea contrives to rush past along parallel highways but in opposite directions. Most sinister of all is a patch of sleek, glossy calm. So what could possibly make sense of all that?

The question is no sooner lodged than the sea provides an answer. It comes in the shape of a surfacing dorsal fin of improbably large dimensions, and it cuts a dead straight diagonal through all of the above as if it were as easy as the Caledonian Canal rather than the notorious fragment of the Atlantic Ocean that so torments the south-most thrust of all Scotland. Over there is Cumbria, there the Isle of Man, that low-lying hull is Ireland, and there is what looks like a mountainous island somewhere farther west. Surely that can't be Arran, you ask yourself. You're right, it can't. It's the Mountains of Mourne. This is a tricky place to get your bearings. Unless, of course, you are the dorsal-finned one making a gentle, slicing mockery of the Mull's reputation for menace.

Suddenly there is a second, smaller fin some distance behind the first. I remember the otters, two creatures steaming line-astern and apparently nose-to-tail, and angling inshore towards the relatively sheltered bay directly below; apparently nose-to-tail because the way the second fin slavishly follows the first (albeit with a looser, wavering approach to the straight line) is also suggestive of another almost unthinkable possibility. It is that the two fins belong to the same creature.

The bay's water is completely clear, and into its orbit there sails a thing that will redefine forever any ideas you may have entertained about the word 'fish'. Where you might expect to see a mouth there is a JCB bucket with its jaws wide open. Your eye travels back along the length of the fish to the dorsal fin, which you now see is perhaps a metre tall. The second fin is still some distance away – 10 feet, 15 feet, 20? The light on the water plays tricks, but there is no denying that the beast in the bay is an adult basking shark – 30 feet long, 35 feet, 40?

And yes, it is a fish, and as harmless to you or me as a gold-fish, unless, that is, it chooses to surface under your sea kayak, in which case you might find yourself suddenly airborne and then swimming. It swims with its vast mouth agape to inhale tiny particles by the ton – phytoplankton and other microscopic riches – which it filters from the water via a system of gill rakers as outsized as its mouth.

A particularly vigorous flourish of the smaller fin, (which turns out to be the tip of its tail), sets a new course and the fish curves away from the bay and subsides into distance and deeper water.

Basking sharks crop up mostly in late spring and summer and all up the western seaboard of Scotland, but the Mull of Galloway, the waters off the Isle of Mull, Ardnamurchan and around the Small Isles offer the best chance of seeing them, pre-sumably because there lie the richest feeding waters. I have seen four together off Mull, which I thought must be a rarity, but occasionally, huge shoals of several hundred crop up to astound coast watchers and seafarers.

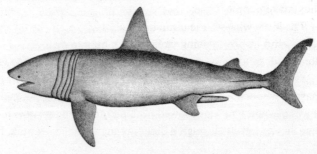

Cetaceans

Conditions that suit basking sharks also work well for the baleen whales. They also sift the minutiae of the ocean, up to and including small fish through baleen plates that line the insides of their mouths instead of teeth. The smallest of the baleens, and the commonest whale of Scottish coastal waters, is the minke, but the showstopper is the humpback. Nothing about it is commonplace. It travels the world singing. Each group of animals has its own 'songs' by which they can be recognised many undersea miles away. These slowly evolve over years, but still they enable reunions with kin at the end of thousand-mile journeys. American biologist Roger Payne has proved that the vocal repertoire of humpbacks really does contain 'songs' complete with repeated patterns of notes and even rhymes.

The humpback is the living proof of the argument that size is everything. When it thrashes the water with its tail (which may be up to 20 feet wide) it achieves the dual effect of stunning a shoal of small fish and galvanising a boatload of camera-toting whale watchers. And when it hurtles from deep below the surface into the air, twists its house-sized bulk through 180 degrees and crashes down again on its back with flailing pectoral fins (up to 15 feet long) so that the ocean rocks, you know you are in the presence of one of nature's superheroes. Or it may just surface and lie quite still, then slowly raise a pectoral fin like an arm, apparently waving, and there is no human resolve that can resist the impulse to raise your arm and wave back. Wherever humpbacks come close to our coasts, they make people smile.

The killer whale is the ultimate symbol of the toothed whales and a kind of ocean-going wolf, a pack hunter with occasional 'lone wolf' tendencies, and the top predator to which pretty well everything else defers. I saw one from the wheelhouse of a two-masted schooner at about 4am en route from St Kilda to Mull. It was my first whale, it showed nothing other than its dorsal fin that sliced steadily through a quiet ocean, about six feet tall. No

other part of the whale showed; no hint of head or back or belly or tail, no suggestion of brute mass or tonnage. There was just that eerie, silent, travelling black cone with no visible means of support or propulsion. Then it was lost among endless waves on a morning of glittering blue beauty that I shared briefly with a bit of a whale.

I turned to the mate at the wheel.

"What is it?" I asked.

"Killer," he said.

It's a terrible name. Yes, it kills. But then so do its cetacean kin, the dolphins and porpoises that so charm us when they play with the bow wave of our boats, and you can build a tourist industry around that as they have done in the Moray Firth.

Roger Payne wrote:

> *People simply don't forget the first time in their lives that they saw a whale. They never tell you, 'Well, I just can't remember whether I've seen a whale or not.' (Or if they do, you know they haven't seen one.)*

No, you never forget your first whale. You never forget the feeling of something other. You never forget the feeling of sensing but not seeing that which is hidden, nor the awareness of a world traveller on the march from ocean to ocean to ocean.

Seals

The bull grey seal has a quizzical smile, as if he possesses secret knowledge. It is a preposterous idea, but for as long as people have been telling stories along the coasts and among the islands of Scotland, they have suffused them with preposterous ideas about seals and invested them with magical powers and human sensibilities. Seals have been established in our collective folk mind and our legend-making for thousands of years as creatures with which we have been willing to change places, a distinction they share with swans. In that spirit, watching a bull grey seal surface 20 yards offshore, you can feel justified in concluding that he has a quizzical smile.

He also has iceberg tendencies. You see the head and the several chins: you do not see the sunk seven-eighths slung vertically beneath the lowest chin. It is a remarkable feat of buoyancy that upholds perhaps 900 pounds of flesh and blubber as easily as if it were a lobster pot float. You believe in it only for as long as you see just the surfacing head, the ripple of chins, the quizzical smile. But see him on his winter battleground, awesome, fat, bloodied and roaring in defence of the right to breed with a harem of females, a berserk rage in his every gesture, spilled blood reddening the surf, then thundering ashore after the battle to reinforce his stature in the eyes of the females and to lick his wounds, and you believe easily in the 900 pounds, but not that the bloodied, bellowing monster might effortlessly float like that disembodied head out there with its ruff of chins, its serene self-containment, and its quizzical smile. Seals are nothing if not deceptive.

They have also been rather carelessly named. There are two species in Scottish waters, the grey or Atlantic seal and the common or harbour seal (it seems two names each are compulsory). The grey seal can be every shade from almost black to chestnut brown and the pups are white, and you can find them on such un-Atlantic shores as Berwickshire and Tentsmuir (see St Andrews, page 188) on the Tay estuary. The common seal is not at all common, and its numbers are mysteriously dwindling, and it harbours no conspicuous affinity for harbours.

And seals have a habit of not conforming to the generalities of field guides that tell you that greys like rocky shores on the west coast and the Hebridean islands and common seals like the sandy shores and offshore sandbanks on the east coast and the northern islands. There are common seals on some very rocky corners of Shetland and nestling in Hebridean waters, and grey seals on the east coast sandbanks of Tentsmuir, which, incidentally, they share with common seals, and the field guides don't tell you about that possibility either.

The Tentsmuir situation is made possible by the sheer amount of sand at the seals' disposal, not just the miles of beach but the long sprawl of offshore sandbanks at Tentsmuir Point, and further low-tide sandbanks that characterise the estuary all the way up to Perth; that and the fact that common seals have their pups in early summer and greys – inexplicably – in early winter. It was here, too, growing up in Dundee across the estuary from Tentsmuir, that I first became accustomed to seals at close quarters, and learned early on to spot the difference between common and grey and their different habits.

We have moved on – uncomfortably recently – from our long history of slaughtering seals literally in their millions, so that they are now the focus of sustained conservation efforts. The process probably began with Frank Fraser Darling's studies on the Treshnish Isles off Mull, and his persuasive writing, such as these lines about one particular bull he christened Old Tawny:

> *His movements ashore were delightful to watch – the way he would make himself comfortable on the rock and then the expressive movements of his forelimbs...you would see Old Tawny scratch his belly delicately with his fingernails, waft a fly from his nose, and then, half closing his hand, draw it down over his face and nose just as men often do. Then he would smooth his whiskers with the back of his hand, this side and*

that...You might see him scratch one palm with the fingers of the other hand, or close his fist and scratch the back of it. A seal's movements are often a most laughable travesty of humanity, but considered more carefully as seal movements, they have great beauty.

And since then, we have advanced to a point at which, with the notable exception of a few fishermen, Scotland disapproves of seal culls. In some places we go further. At Tentsmuir, for example, signs urge visitors to watch the seals from a distance to avoid distress to the females and their pups. When you think about it, a sign asking us to be considerate in the company of seals is a fair measure of how far we have travelled in our relationship with the natural world.

It is April. At the furthest edge of the sand you see what looks at first glance like a slowly breaking wave, except that it is dark brown while every other wave is grey-green unfurling to white, except that the wave neither advances nor retreats, although it most definitely moves. It is a restless wave of 300 to 400 grey seals, but if you were looking for a single word to characterise the creature in front of you, you certainly wouldn't reach for 'grey', not with the sun on that almost orangey female that appears to be fanning herself with her own tail at the centre of the group, or that off-white youngster, or that one right on the extreme edge that looks coal-black against the light. Nor would you reach for 'Atlantic', not on this Europe-facing shore of the land. You might think about 'long-nosed', or you might think about 'singing', for these are qualities both associated with the species. Indeed, it is the siren-song of the grey seal that is at the heart of the Scottish selkie tradition, the voice of the enchantress within that seduces deluded young men.

A dozen nimble little waders – turnstones – run in among the seals, and even appear to be finding food on the seals' bodies. But why turnstones alone, of all the wader tribes that throng all the seal coasts, have identified a seal colony as a source of food, and are tolerated by the seals at such intimately close quarters...that is just one more unsolved seal mystery, that and the secret knowledge that lies behind the quizzical smile of the grey bull, that and what a turnstone finds to eat in his copious midriff.

Seabirds

From Tentsmuir to Ardnamurchan, from Berwickshire to Sutherland, and from Shetland to the Mull of Galloway, the coasts of Scotland throb with the lives of birds from sanderlings to sea eagles, from gannets to guillemots, and from plovers to puffins. For me, the particular charm of coastal birds is their voices, which are always heard against the eternally unfinished symphony of waves. So I seek out (in no particular order of preference and in no particular combination) the uillean pipes of curlew, the creamy whoop of eider drakes, the percussive triplets of kittiwakes, the yodelling of long-tailed ducks, the diminuendo trill of redshanks, the reedy legato of red-throated divers that once lulled me to sleep in a tent on Raasay and roused me from sleep six hours later. Ah, you had to be there.

At its most blatant, the spectacle contrives blizzards of gannets crash-diving the shoals while the great skuas – bonxies – go in among them like handsome thugs and bully them out of their catch in mid-air or on the surface before they can take off. At its most furtive, it is a solitary, meticulously camouflaged purple sandpiper silently scavenging in a low-tide bed of seaweed that wears exactly the same shades of nondescript plumage, all of which rather makes you wonder why nature gave the sandpiper such vivid yellow legs.

On the huge seabird cliffs of the north or the great set-piece gannetries of the Bass Rock (see Plants, page 64) or Ailsa Craig (see Ayr, page 207) the sheer numbers of birds, the sheer volume of so many open throats, and the sheer chaos of so much nest-building and mating and fishing and fighting and fetching and carrying is a phenomenon to supercharge even the meekest, the geekiest birdwatcher with flood tides of raw energy. As the season progresses and the eggs hatch any one of those colonies bears witness a thousand times a day to the tiny tragedies inflicted by marauding black-backed gulls, skuas, peregrine falcons and sea eagles. By autumn, the nesting cliffs are ghost towns; the birds have scattered in their hundreds and thousands far across the world's oceans. In their place, the great firths and quiet beaches transform under the invasion of hordes of waders, geese, ducks, and swans from the far north of the world and from the colder landmass of continental Europe. These arrivals and departures and all their rituals are among the most elemental of natural events, moving to the essential rhythms by which nature orchestrates life along the edges of our small portion of the planet.

Sometimes it is easier to make sense of it all by homing in on a single moment of a single bird life, the better to imbue the sense of wonder with a dash of understanding. There was, for example, a brilliant and billowing morning after a night of storm

Plate 113.

on an Orcadian headland and I wanted to walk forever, for the walking had become not just a means of moving but a means of seeing, sensing, scenting, tasting, hearing. A cliff-top skylark rose from a tussock and rose and rose. George Mackay Brown, poet of this place, wrote it down thus: *"A lark splurges in Galilees of sky"*

And with that splurge in my ears I was buoyant and enthralled by the unstoppable vitality of that coast.

The headland climbed to a blunt, bald summit, all but grass-less and burnished by wind. I sat on a small ledge where wind and rain and time had cracked open the skin of the headland and dropped a piece of its slope perhaps 20 inches, leaving a bare brown step of rock and earth. The headland's crouch at my back bore the wind's brunt. Far seas sparkled white amid their deep, dark blues. I unpacked lunch and as I did so I realised I had been there before – right there, on that precise ledge, unpacking lunch. It was the previous June, but I had come on the place from a different direction sauntering south down the Yesnaby coast. I suppose I had climbed the headland for the same rea-sons and found the same ledge. And I had been there for ten minutes when I realised I was not alone, for there was an eye, black and watchful and close to the ground a dozen yards away. It took a few moments of intense scrutiny to define the shape that accommodated the eye, but at last it materialised from its impressive camouflage into an eider duck sitting on her nest, a sumptuous cushion fashioned from her own plucked breast down and therefore precisely the same shades of brown as the rest of her and these perfectly matched the shades of brown of the ledge. She was quite alone: the ledge offered her perfect shelter from sea winds and she had no intention of moving. I gathered my partly-eaten lunch into my pack, photographed her twice, wished her a successful nesting and a long life, and I left.

And now, not quite a year later, I had chanced on the same ledge from the opposite direction. And now, I examined the ground and puzzled over her choice of nest site. The sea, by the shortest route, was up the headland a few yards then over the edge of a 300-feet cliff. The longer route, by which she would have to lead her brood as soon as they could walk to the safety of the sea and a protective crèche of other non-breeding eiders, was a quarter of a mile of steep slope and foreshore without a scrap of shelter to thwart the bonxies and the big gulls. Still, doubtless she had her reasons, doubtless she too had secret knowledge of her own that reinforced them. I wondered how she had fared last year, and whether, a month or two from now, she would fly up from the sea, put down on the slope beside me, cross it to the old familiar security of the ledge, and without pausing to admire the view, begin to pluck at her own breast feathers.

And then, by way of one final example, there is the Arctic tern. If I were to anoint one creature to symbolise the Scottish coast as I anointed Gavin Maxwell to be its laureate, I would choose the Arctic tern, which thinks nothing of flying 10,000 miles for the privilege of nesting here. Its bouncing, waltzing flight looks altogether too flimsy for globetrotting, but there is no bird so devoted to the inexorable. Only the march of time can outlast its capacity for single-mindedness. I watched one for an hour fishing alone late on a June evening above a flat calm sea that faded from palest blue to milk white, and a dozen years after the event I still hold it to be the single most beautiful and the most moving thing I have ever seen.

A couple of years later I found the remains of one on Fair Isle in what had been a disastrous year for those seabirds that depend – as the Arctic tern does – on the migration of sand eels. There were none that year and tern breeding was almost a complete failure, a pointed reminder of the interconnectedness of everything in nature. This particular tern was probably starving when it was killed. I wrote it this epitaph:

The Beautiful Coat

> From crib to coffin
> you must dance in a beautiful coat.
> – George Mackay Brown

Ten thousand miles to nest on Fair Isle
but the sand eels didn't come
and you died, tern, instead. At the end
there were only wing points,
tattered tail streamers,
broken body, severed head,

scarlet mandibles twisted
by the final battle.
But there is this, tern:

you died where you were born
and all your life was a dance
in a beautiful coat.

Jim Crumley

THREE

COASTAL
PLANTS

If you are attuned to plants, even the flash of a slightly different shade of pink in a wayside verge as you drive to the seaside will signal something worth investigating. Not everyone has this level of interest or way of perceiving. It comes from having looked at plants, even if only in an amateur way, since childhood. Maybe it's birds and mammals rather than plants that really fire you, but the fact you are reading this chapter suggests you have some interest in looking at wild flowers and appreciating them where they grow. It is not intended for botanists, but for those of us who are pleased to see flowers and would like to know their names and a little more about them.

Scotland's coasts offer some of the richest grasslands in the UK. What we lose from our northerly latitude and relative paucity of base-rich soils, we gain in having less invasive farming at the margins of our land. The national specialist botanical organisation, Plantlife, has a national list of sites they call 'Important Plant Areas' (IPAs). The designation is not legally binding but is intended to promote public awareness of rich eco-systems and encourage their long-term conservation. Of more than 50 coastal IPAs, only 18 of them are in Scotland but when you see what is designated, you discover it is immensely large areas. Almost the whole of the north coast, a very long stretch of the west coast, and the whole of many islands, from Cumbrae and Colonsay, to mainland Orkney and Shetland, Arran, Rum and most of the Outer Hebrides are considered to be IPAs. Between these the whole range of coastal habitat is covered: cliffs and rocks, dunes, shingle, estuaries and mudflats, and the machair, unique to Scotland and Ireland.

This chapter looks briefly at each of these habitats and tries to describe what you might find on a summer's walk, mentioning also what would be apparent earlier and later in the year. There is not enough space to cover everything, nor even to picture all of those plants that do get a mention. The intention is to offer an interesting and typical selection of seaside plants.

BEACH, DUNE AND COASTAL WOODS

Dunes

Scotland's coasts are frequently rocky, windswept and wave-lashed but there are still plenty of dunes to explore, those behind East Lothian beaches being particularly accessible to many people from the Central Belt. The Arisaig coastal strip is another dune area to be enjoyed (see Arisaig, page 199). The wider the strip of dune between sea and agricultural land, the more likely it is that the landward side will have been stabilised by the growth of plants. In some cases this has been achieved by deliberate planting of species like sea buckthorn (see Foraging, page 70) or marram grass, the tall harsh grass familiar on so many sites from the car park to the tideline. Where the process is natural, various different plant communities can develop. Nettles crop up where people have literally left their mark: in nitrogen-rich environments, and docks will abound in most places, sometimes with members of the nightshade family such as bittersweet, a purple-flowered and red berried shrubby plant. Frequently, sea bindweed *(above)* will trail its striking pink and white striped flowers across the path. If the soil is acid, maritime heath develops, often with a grey coating of lichens covering much of the ground surface. If there are more alkaline conditions the moisture-holding dips or gulleys called 'dune slacks' can form, making remarkable reservoirs for a wide range of wild flowers.

Bird's foot trefoil

Members of the pea family can often be found in such dunes. Gorse and broom may be there and the same yellow vetches that occur in machair (see below, page 58), kidney vetch, bird's foot trefoil *(above)*, and the smaller, clover-flowered black medick, are all quite frequent. Purple milk vetch is easy to miss and, although considered to be threatened, is probably more common on dunes than people think. The much more exotic-looking wood vetch, with its delicately pencilled upper petals is rare but exciting to find, on cliffs and rocky places as well as occasionally on dunes. The long spikes of dark blue flowers of tufted vetch, familiar from hedgerows everywhere, are quite common, and sometimes the more unusual bitter vetch. This plant has broader, more pea-like leaves than the other vetches mentioned, with sprays of four or five flowers that start red and turn more blue as they age, finally becoming yellowy. It used to be a very significant resource in Scotland, chewed like gum to fend off hunger, or added to bootleg whisky to give it some flavour. That flavour is all in the root tubers, making it impossible to experiment with it legally, since it would involve uprooting the plant. There are not enough bitter vetches around to suggest this is ever a good idea, although they do grow on heath land as well as dunes. A more compact pea is the little rest harrow (the name comes from 'resist' harrow, as it was a common weed of cultivation), with pink flowers on short, wiry, leafy stems. It is summer flowering and should not be confused with lousewort, a plant with similar pink flowers but a member of a different family. This flowers earlier, though you might find it in similar places. A relative of lousewort is yellow rattle *(below)*, common on stabilised sand dunes. This plant is semi-parasitic on grass roots, so is a useful addition to any wild flower seed mix as it helps to prevent grasses from becoming dominant. The main suppliers of wild seeds, such as Scotia Seeds, sell it, so there is no need to deplete the sand dunes of their seed stocks.

Yellow rattle

A large pink-flowered plant you might come across on dunes could be common mallow, although it is confined to the south of Scotland. An even larger yellow-flowered plant you might encounter could be evening primrose. It is not native but has become naturalised in places like some of the East Lothian

Viper's-bugloss

dunes. The tall spikes produce a series of single, bell-shaped blossoms that only come out fully towards evening. Each lasts only one day but every evening from June to September brings a new flower opening within a group of plants. A large and notable blue-flowered plant is sea holly. Very unusual in Scotland but sometimes found in the south-west and in the Western Isles, it is an extremely handsome plant with prickly grey leaves and balls of thistle-like flowers, each of which has a ruff of prickles. The roots taste spicy, like galangal (related to ginger) and used to be candied and eaten as sweets. More commonly come across is viper's-bugloss (*above*), an upright plant with bristly stems and blue flowers that have a pink tinge about them. On the strand-line, large clumps of branchy, radish-like plants with pale pink stock-like flowers may be sea rocket.

In the context of sand dunes, though more likely to be found on stable beaches with a good ridge of sand and shingle, are some of the edible maritime plants mentioned in the foraging chapter. Sea kale, sea beet, and silverweed (see page 60, pages 102–103) are all to be seen, although only the last is widespread and common on dunes. Orache, another member of the spin-ach family which can be eaten, grows on dunes and on the strand-line. In the past people were discouraged from gathering it and similar species, for fear of coastal erosion. The old time gatherers of lady's bedstraw *(below)*, who used the roots for dye, almost certainly did cause erosion in places.

Lady's bedstraw

Beaches

Stable beaches that support plant communities are not frequent but there are a few interesting exceptions. The Culbin Sands near Forres are a large area of sand dune that used to be extremely unstable until much of it was planted with commercial conifers, starting in the 19th century and continuing into the present day. The sands are still shifted by storms, causing problems to the Forestry Commission, which manages the trees, but the wholesale movement has been arrested, so both beach and dune communities of plants can be observed.

The long beach at Culbin has patches of shingle that support maritime heathland species, like juniper, crowberry and heathers. It is surprising to see them almost at sea level. Near them you may come across oyster plant, a prostrate member of the borage family, with snaking stems up to 50cm long and undivided, blue-grey fleshy leaves. The flowers are small and bell-shaped, reddish when young, becoming blue as they develop. The name comes from Shetlanders who claim the plant tastes like oysters. It certainly has a slippery texture that might remind you of shellfish but the mild flavour has nothing but a touch of cucumber about it. For all that, it is an interesting plant to find and looks as if it might be an exotic, escaped from a garden.

Further up the beach and into the dune system, all sorts of special and appealing flowers bloom in the summer. Sea centaury has a slender greyish stem bearing a cluster of two or three starry pink flowers. Eyebright, a small, upright plant with lobed white or purplish flowers, is common, and with it two species of milkwort *(below)*, with blue, pink or white spears of tiny blossoms. It is related to garden veronicas.

Milkwort

Coastal woods

No mention of Culbin would be complete without reference to the plants to be found within the woods. This damp environment harbours some rarities such as coralroot orchid, with an eerie, yellowy-green stem that arises, leafless, from the forest floor and bears equally strange little flowers with a white central lobe and lop-ears of the same yellow hue as the stem. More showy is single-flowered wintergreen with its waxy, white, five-petalled flowers on slender stalks, arising from creeping stems with leaves

Twinflower

not unlike those of violets. Study individual blossoms because they are exquisite: a trio of stamens with pollen-bearing anthers sits on each petal, with a spectacular, bulbous stigma at their centre. Another rare and exciting plant you might see is twinflower *(above)*, an iconic species of Caledonian pinewoods. Its two pinkish, bell-shaped flowers are displayed at the top of a slender stalk, which, like all these specialist woodland species just described, is leafless.

MACHAIR

Machair is really a form of low dune, unique to Scotland and Ireland, but better represented in the Hebrides than anywhere else. It is probably our greatest botanical glory. The sheer profusion of species in bloom on machair makes it profoundly different from the cropped grasslands we are used to. It is richer than moorland, more varied than sea-cliff grassland, and more colourful than any other native habitat.

The word is Gaelic, and means 'fertile plain' in a more general sense than we now understand by machair. The definition of machair as a distinctive habitat has been refined in the past 80 years or so. It refers to coastal areas with large deposits of broken shell that have blown there over millennia. The areas are mostly flat and can be distinguished from dunes by their lower content of sand. Consisting of up to 80% shell, machair soils are alkaline and therefore support special vegetation that is unusual in Scotland, where acid soils are more common. The combination of the shell-rich soil and the wild, wet weather of the west coast partly account for this type of grassland, but without controlled grazing they would cease to be quite so remarkably rich in flowers. With agricultural changes, such grazing is no longer assured, so maintaining the machair is becoming a problem that has to be embraced by environmental organisations which can see the value of preserving their wealth.

Opposite: marsh marigold;
Top row (l to r): buttercup, eyebright, clover;
Middle row (l to r): ragged robin, harebell, sheepsbit scabious;
Bottom row (l to r): devilsbit scabious, greater butterfly orchid, gentian.

If you wander into machair in late June or July you will be aware of a sweet smell, a lively dance of colour, and on a still day, the noise of insects. In the early season the predominant colour is yellow. Primroses and marsh marigolds are some of the first plants to flower, followed by several species of buttercups, then kidney vetch, birdsfoot trefoil, lady's bedstraw, and by the middle of summer, silverweed, corn marigolds and yellow rattle. A little later clovers, both red and white, starts to bloom and it is their smell that fills the air. Sailors are said to have been able to smell land before they could see it and, on a warm day in the machair, the delicious scents of the flower meadow are so strong that it is easy to believe they wafted far out to sea.

Ragged robin and spotted orchids add their pinks to the mixture of colours, and several different vetches, harebells and forget-me-nots, some touches of blue. Late in the season this is amplified by sheepsbit and devilsbit scabious, both of which can flower right into the autumn. Lower-growing plants like eyebright, wild thyme, and sea milkwort give an under-storey to the jungle of flowers. According to Plantlife up to 45 species of plant can be found in a single square metre of machair on the Uists, which hold some of the very best examples of this remarkable habitat.

Within the riot of bright but relatively familiar flowers, some rarities crop up. You might happen on one of a whole range of orchids such as frog orchid, lesser and greater butterfly orchid, marsh orchid, pyramidal orchid and tway-blade. Members of the gentian family are other interesting plants to look out for, although it is the purple-coloured field gentian or felwort that you are more likely to see than the clear blue spring gentian. Within the machair of the north coast, you might see mountain avens, a tiny shrub with pretty, short-stemmed white flowers, each with a golden centre of stamens. It has small, crinkly-edged leaves and belongs to the rose family.

CLIFFS AND ROCKY SHORES

If you walk cliff tops in spring you are likely to see primroses, which survive even in sheep pasture because they are relatively unpalatable. Celandines, dog violets, golden saxifrage (*above*) and later, bluebells abound in many places all round the coast. If they are present with species like the delicate-stemmed pinkish-white wood anemone or lusty dark green clumps of wood rush, it may indicate the place was formerly wooded. On the west coast, especially in Sunart and Ardnamurchan, it may still be wooded, predominately with hazel, which give a good spring show of lambs-tail catkins, and willows. Catkins of the latter mature at different times over several months, according to which of the many species is present. These western woods are fragments of our own native temperate rainforest, and can be extremely rich in mosses, lichens, ferns and liverworts. The Sunart oakwoods, rising above the shore, are a fine example.

Certain more limey cliff top woods, like those above the Moray Firth between Rosemarkie and Shandwick, are home to rarer species like the little silver-leaved rock whitebeam. Related to the very familiar rowan, it has similar flowers followed by rather more squat red berries. In the same area you may see juniper, more familiar from inland sites. Growing among such shrubs, honeysuckle abounds in many places, adding a profusion of flowers to cliff woodland. Wild roses, particularly the downy rose, with its deep pink flowers in summer and bright, hairy, rounded hips in autumn, and the burnet rose (*below*), white flowered, with neat serrated-edged leaves, and bearing black hips, are not uncommon.

Burnet rose

Most of these species can be viewed from below, or from the occasional path up a cliff. As you leave the beach in summer you are very likely to see the pink flowering tufts of sea thrift. It is a salt-loving plant that can grow on rocks only just above the splash-line as well as higher on cliffs. In recent years it has appeared beside well-salted highways, notably the A9 south of Inverness, where gritters have created something resembling a maritime environment. Near it you may well come across sea campion, a short relative of red campion, with white flowers and papery bladders protecting its seed pods. Both these plants can start to flower early in sunny years but beating them into bloom will be the little blue spring squill, a native that looks as if it has escaped from a garden. Cliff tops in the Hebrides and on the north and west coasts can sometimes abound in these little scillas. Flowering later, in May and June, and restricted to well-drained grassland, usually near coasts, in Orkney, Caithness and Sutherland, is the Scottish primrose (often known by its Latin name, *Primula scotica*). This is one of Scotland's few endemic (meaning that it is only found here) species. It has short, multi-headed stems with pinkish-purple flowers, and a rosette of green leaves that are grey and mealy beneath. Don't expect anything as large as a regular primrose, as the plants stand only a few centimetres high, making them hard to spot until you get your eye adjusted to them. It is a special treat to find them.

If you find yourself on cliffs with good grassland that is not over-grazed, you may discover flowers in great profusion and variety. Fragrant agrimony lives up to its name although its relative with a similar spike of small yellow flowers, common agrimony (*below*), has no smell at all. Many of the species that are common on machair may also appear, depending on the aspect, exposure and nature of the soils. If you take your cliff top walk in the middle of summer you will soon know whether you have a wild flower haven or not.

Agrimony

Tree mallow is an introduced cliff species that infests some seabird nesting sites, notably the Bass Rock and Craigleith island in the Firth of Forth. It enjoys the guano-enriched soils in these places but in recent years has multiplied to such an extent that puffins cannot find sites to burrow without encountering its roots, and even gannets are having trouble in finding nest sites. Tree mallows can be up to 3m tall and shaped rather like large brussel sprout plants with thick stems that tend to lose their lower big, five-lobed, leaves. The flowers are shallow pink trumpets with a dark purple centre, like those of the garden lavatera to which it is related. Where these plants are a problem, volunteers are stepping in to help manage them. They are obliged to cut stems several times a year to stop new growth. It is estimated that this regime will have to be maintained for many years to come in order to rid these islands of the invasive mallow. It has been around for at least 300 years, although it has only latterly become a problem. A warming climate may account for its recent proliferation.

Another introduced plant you might encounter on Firth of Forth cliffs, especially island ones, is Alexanders (see Foraging, page 101). Scots lovage (see Foraging, page 101) is a native, you are more likely to see on northern cliffs and in rocky places below them. As well as being eaten as a vegetable, it used to be valued as a cure-all. Rock samphire (see Foraging, page 100) is also native, but not common, even in the south-west. All of these are members of the carrot family, the first two having broad, glossy leaves. The samphire, however, has narrowly divided leaves of a rather distinctive grey-green that are fleshy, like so many seaside species.

ESTUARY AND SALTMARSH

The marshy fringes of estuaries may not be everyone's choice for a seaside walk but they are rich in wildlife. Birdwatchers in particular frequent them, though they not only abound in birds, but also in a range of unusual plants. Some, like the yellow flag, are familiar from other marshy environments but many others are adapted to living in very salty conditions. A typical adaptation is fleshy leaves. These seem to make it possible for such plants to survive inundation by high tides, even though their preferred niche is just above the tideline.

One strange plant thrives in a zone that is submerged and exposed again by daily tides. This is eelgrass, not one of the seaweeds (which are algae rather than 'higher plants') but a flowering plant. It is bright green and flat-leaved like meadow grass, but the leaves are less rigid so that they can wave in the water. There are three species of eelgrass. They are not common around Scotland but if you visit the Dornoch Firth you might encounter at least two of them.

Along the higher part of an estuarine shore you will find those salt-adapted plants. Shrubby sea-blite looks a little like a rosemary bush with more succulent leaves that vary from dark green to reddish. Its smaller relative, annual sea-blite *(above, left)*, tends to be brighter green and have the appearance of miniature branches of Christmas tree. Its growth can be luxurious. Near it, particularly in silty places, you might encounter samphire, also called glasswort (see Foraging, page 99). Other relatively common species are sea purslane, the leaves of which are not so much succulent as grey and leathery, and sea aster *(previous page, right)*, which looks like a shorter, more fleshy-leaved version of Michaelmas daisy. Where there is sand as well as silt, sea sandwort, with its reddish creeping shoots that support an abundance of bright green, crisp, broad but pointed leaves can be found. They are tipped with small starry flowers. Sea sandwort is reminiscent of certain succulents commercially available, so tends to catch the eye. Another little plant that shows the saline conditions adaptation is sea milkwort. Unlike its cousins, the blue, white or purple milkworts that occur in sand dunes as well as further inland, the sea species has a leafy flower spike and pink flowers.

Sea lavender *(illustrated on the chapter-opening page)*, the prettiest plant of the saltmarsh, only occurs in southern Scotland, so you might encounter it on the coast of Dumfries and Galloway or along very restricted parts of the East Lothian coast. The 'saltings' or 'grassland with pools' type of saltmarsh that it favours is a picturesque habitat, confined now mostly to the Solway coast, since similar land around the Firth of Forth was drained long ago. Such pool systems, connected by creeks, and sometimes by underground natural 'pipes', is challenging country to cross as channels too wide to jump are frequently encountered. The ground is often saturated and consequently very fragile, so tread lightly on it or view it from a made path or causeway.

Coastal Plants

LIST OF SCOTLAND'S COMMONLY SEEN COASTAL PLANTS

ENGLISH NAME	LATIN NAME	GAELIC NAME
marram grass	*Ammophila arenaria*	*muran*
*bittersweet / poison berry	*Solanum dulcemara*	*searbhag mhilis*
sea bindweed	*Calystegia sodlanella*	*flùr a' phrionnsa*
gorse	*Ulex europaeus*	*conasg*
broom	*Cytisus scorparius*	*bealaidh*
*kidney vetch	*Anthyllis vulneraria*	*cas an uain*
birds foot trefoil	*Lotus corniculatus*	*peasair a' mhadaidh-raidh*
*black medick	*Medicago lupulina*	*dubh-mheidig*
*wood vetch	*Vicia sylvatica*	*peasair coille*
*tufted vetch	*Vicia cracca*	*peasair nan luch*
*bitter vetch	*Lathyrus linifolius*	*carra meille*
*restharrow	*Ononis repens*	*sreang bogha*
*lousewort	*Pedicularis sylvatica*	*lus riabhach monaidh*
*yellow rattle	*Rhinanthus minor*	*bodach nan claigeann*
mallow	*Lavatera sylvestris*	*ucas fiadhain*
tree mallow	*Lavatera arbora*	*ucas àrd*
*evening primrose	*Oenothera biennis*	*coinneal oidhche*
*viper's bugloss	*Echium vulgare*	*lus na nathrach*
*sea holly	*Eryngium maritimum*	*cuileann tràgha*
juniper	*Juniperus communis*	*aiteann*
crowberry	*Empetrum nigrum*	*lus na feannaig*
heather	*Calluna vulgaris*	*fraoch*
*oyster plant	*Mertensia maritime*	*tiodhlac na mara*
*single-flowered wintergreen	*Moneses uniflora*	*glas-luibh chùbhraidh*
*twinflower	*Linnea borealis*	*lus Linneuis*
*coralroot orchid	*Corallorhiza trifida*	*freumh corail*
*sea centuary	*Centuarium eyrthraea*	*ceud bhileach*
eyebright	*Euphrasia officinalis*	*soillse nan sùl*
milkwort	*Polygala vulgaris*	*siabann nam ban-sìth*
*lady's bedstraw	*Galium verum*	*lus an leasaich*
primrose	*Primula vulgaris*	*sòbhrag*
*celandine	*Ranunculus ficaria*	*searragaich*
*golden saxifrage	*Chrysosplenium oppositifolium*	*lus nan laogh*
woodrush	*Luzula campestris*	*learman raoin*
bluebell	*Endymion non-scriptus*	*bròg na cuthaig*
dog violet	*Viola canina*	*sàil-chuach mòintich*
hazel	*Corylus avellana*	*calltainn*
willows	*Salix spp*	*seileach*
*buttercup	*Ranunculus spp*	*buidheag*

*marsh marigold	*Caltha palustris*	*lus buidhe bealltainn*
*corn marigold	*Chrysanthemum segetum*	*bile bhuidhe*
*sea mayweed	*Tripleurospermum maritimum*	*buidheag na mara*
red clover	*Trifolium pratense*	*seamrag dhearg*
white clover	*Trifolium repens*	*seamrag bhàn*
*ragged robin	*Lychnis flos-cuculi*	*caorag lèana*
forget-me-not	*Myosotis spp*	*lus midhe*
*sheepsbit	*Jasione montana*	*putan gorm*
devilsbit scabious	*Succisa pratensis*	*grèim an diabhail*
harebell	*Campanula rotundifolia*	*currac cuthaig*
*wild thyme	*Thymus serpyllum*	*lus mhic rìgh Bhreatainn*
*field gentian	*Gentianella campestris*	*lus a' chrùbain*
spotted orchid	*Dactylorhiza fuchsia*	*urach bhallach*
*mountain avens	*Dryas octopetala*	*machall monaidh*
honeysuckle	*Lonicera periclymenum*	*lus na meala*
*burnet rose	*Rosa pimpernellifolia*	*ròs beag ban na h-Alba*
*downy rose	*Rosa tomentosa*	
*Eel grass	*Zostera marina*	*milearach*
*sea thrift	*Armeria maritima*	*tonn a' chladaich*
red campion	*Silene dioicia*	*cìrean coilich*
*sea campion	*Silene uniflora*	*coirean na mara*
*Scottish primrose	*Primula scotica*	*sòbhrag Albannach*
*spring squill	*Scilla verna*	*lear-uinnean*
*sea lavender	*Limonium vulgare*	*lus na tùise mara*
*sea sandwort	*Honckenya peploides*	*lus a' ghoill*
*sea milkwort	*Glaux maritima*	*lus na saillteachd*
*sea aster	*Aster tripolium*	*neòinean sàilein*
*sea purslane	*Halimione portulcoides*	
*sea rocket	*Cakile maritime*	*fearsaideag*
shrubby sea blite	*Suaeda vera*	*praiseach na mara*
annual sea blite	*Suaeda maritima*	
*early marsh orchid	*Dactylorhiza incarnate*	*mogairlean lèana*
*frog orchid	*Coeloglossum viride*	*mogairlean losgainn*
*greater butterfly orchid	*Platanthera chlorantha*	*mogairlean an dealain-dè mòr*
Irish lady's tresses	*Spiranthes romanzoffiana*	*mogairlean bachlach bàn*
fragrant agrimony	*Agrimonia procera*	*geur-bhileach chùbhraidh*
*flag iris	*Iris pseudacorus*	

*Species marked * are illustrated in the colour plates section.*

FOUR

COASTAL BOUNTY

The seaside is a good place to forage. The species that brought our early ancestors to live by the shore are still there. Shellfish have somehow survived oil-spills and long-term commercial harvesting (now declining) and are still a resource. Certain species of seaweed are among the few plants you can harvest in Scotland during winter months. Sea buckthorn berries are another. Commonly known as 'the baked bean bush' they are easy to identify along eastern dunes.

If you plan to take anything to eat that has been in sea water, be scrupulous about examining the proposed gathering site before you do so. Shellfish in particular, and seaweed too, can very easily pick up contamination from a variety of different sources such as sewage outflows (including from private septic tanks), industrial pollution, river water which contains either of those things, and possibly even radiation from nearby nuclear power stations. Check the Scottish Environmental Protection Agency (SEPA) website for their list of clean bathing beaches. This is a good start, but use your own eyes and local information as well.

Food is not the only resource that can be foraged. The sea yields all manner of useful things, from wrecks (providential for struggling fishing communities in the past) to wrack and other seaweeds that can be collected as fertiliser. Sometimes, as Compton Mackenzie memorably recorded, it has yielded whisky.

In this chapter we will look first at foraged food, and then at the potential for gleaning and gathering along the Scottish coasts. Beachcombing, despite the depressing mountains of plastic you will encounter, still holds the thrill of the unexpected.

Before you start

Basic precautions

- If you are gathering on cliffs, be aware of possible erosion and crumbling. Do not get too close to the edge.
- Be aware of tide times and ensure that you're not at risk of being cut off by the incoming tide.
- Don't walk along cliffs or rocky coastlines in high winds or gusts.
- Don't walk out over muddy or estuarine sands, where you might get trapped in sticky mud or quicksand. Ask locally about safety before venturing out.
- Wear suitable footwear to avoid injury from rocks, barnacles, shells, crabs, stinging creatures or even litter.
- If you're beachcombing alone, make sure you've told someone where you are and when you expect to return. Don't rely on your mobile phone unless you know your phone gets a good signal where you're foraging.

Conservation basics

- Only take small quantities of any plants, shellfish or seaweeds, and check individual species to find out which are protected or too scarce to take at all.
- When you turn over rocks, return them to exactly where they were to avoid destroying delicate habitats. Be careful not to squash surfaced creatures when you do so.

Gathering equipment

Strong plastic bags for collecting, and a stout stick to help you over the rocks (and whisk a crab from its hole) are the essential items for beach foraging. A bucket can also be useful for storing live creatures, or just for viewing them before you return them to the water. The different types of net needed for shrimps and prawns are discussed in the relevant sections.

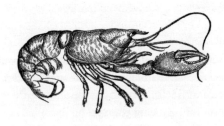

SHELLFISH

CRABS AND LOBSTERS

Lobsters, *Homarus gammarus vulgaris*, usually live below the low-tide mark, so only the very lowest of spring tides is likely to reveal them. You would be a very lucky forager to find one and bring it home without risking your fingers succumbing to its powerful claws!

Shore crabs, *Carcinas maenas*, are the most commonly found crustaceans. Brown or beige, and attractively marked when young, their smooth shells are usually green when fully grown and are about 6 to 8cm long. Although small children find it endlessly exciting to excavate them from sandy pools, or to catch them on baited lines, they aren't edible. Hold them, let tiny ones scuttle on your hand, and put them back to live, and perhaps feed something else.

Edible crabs, *Cancer pagurus*, grow larger, up to about 20cm when mature. The dusky pink shell is roughly oval and is indented like a pie crust. The ends of its claws are black. The crab used to be familiar enough from fishmongers' displays, although many now sell crab meat in plastic pots rather than returned to the inverted shell.

Edible crabs live in deeper water than shore crabs, so you need a low tide, preferably a spring tide, for it to be worth hunting them. Wait until the tide is almost at its lowest, then seek them in whatever pools have been left by the retreating sea. They like to lie up in crevices, or under stones. Flick seaweed aside to reveal them, or lift stones neatly and swiftly. It's best to have two people on the job: one lifting and one looking. Beware the crabs in cracks. Don't try to pick them out with your hand as they can exert extraordinary force by pushing with their legs. There are stories of people being trapped by them and caught by the incoming tide. Use a stick (and always watch for the tide turning). Old timers make the crab latch its claws on to the stick, and then whip the creature out.

Velvet swimming crabs, *Necora puber*, are another edible species that live in deeper water. On the west coast they can be abundant just below the low-tide line. They are from about 6cm to a maximum of 12cm across the shell, reddish brown, with blue joints and lines on their hairy legs. Look for them on the lowest spring tides. They inhabit the areas thick with oarweed, and other large seaweeds, and can be found by flicking these aside. They scuttle away, so you will have to move fast. Beware their claws as they are quite aggressive. Velvets are harder work to prepare than their larger cousins but they taste sweet and good. You can sometimes acquire them from crab boats if you ask in advance, as the fishermen usually throw them back.

Common spider crabs, *Maja squinado*, is a further edible species you might encounter in the same low tidal zone as edible and velvet swimming crabs. These crabs are reddish pink, with heart-shaped bodies, long legs, have hard spines all round the edge of their shells, and smaller ones covering the entire top surface. They are such extraordinary creatures you may want just to look at them rather than take them home for the pot.

You should not keep any crab if it is in the process of renewing its armour and is soft-shelled (it will not taste good and the texture will be poor), if it is carrying eggs, or if it is too small. There is plenty of legislation surrounding the size of crabs and other shellfish that may be removed, but this varies locally and changes from time to time. For brown crabs, for example, the legal size limit for crabs you may remove is 14cm across the broadest part of the carapace for those caught north of 56 degrees (the latitude that runs just north of Edinburgh on the east, and south of Lochgilphead on the west) and 13cm for any caught south of that.

To handle your crab, grasp it longitudinally along the top of the shell, watching out for the claws. Carry it home in a pail or plastic box. It will live for several hours out of water but it is best to put it out of its misery quickly. The humane way is to put it in the freezer for 2 to 3 hours to make it comatose. Remove the animal from the freezer and turn it upside down, making sure as you do so that it is unconscious (no eye movements). Take a sharp, thin knife, lift the tail flap and stab it where you can see a small depression or hole. Now stab it in the shallow depression near the crab's mouth. This will kill the crab by destroying its two nerve centres. It's nasty work but honest: if we are to enjoy meat of any sort, we have to accept that animals need to be killed. Clearly it ought to be done humanely, and the traditional way of chucking a crab into boiling water causes it suffering. This method spares them that.

Next weigh the crab, as the boiling time depends on its size. It will need 15 minutes for the first half kilo, then 10 minutes for each successive half kilo. The water should be strongly salted, with about 100g in 2 litres: according to Jane Grigson,

a whole uncooked egg should be able to float in the brine. Remove from the water as soon as cooking is complete and allow the crab to cool. When it is cold, put it upside down on the table and have beside you some newspaper, a couple of bowls, a small sharp knife, a mallet, a dessert spoon, and a teaspoon. Twist off the legs and set aside. Then tear off the tail flap and prise away the bony underside of the body. You will see the gills, or 'dead men's fingers'. Discard these and use your spoon to scoop out the soft, brownish meat from the shell, putting it into one of the bowls. You may be able to glean some of this meat from the central body part as well. Next wrap a claw in newspaper and gently hit it with a mallet, trying to crack it rather than smash it. Remove the white meat from the claws with your fingers and the teaspoon. Children can be good at this job, and more persistent than adults. It's possible to winkle meat out of crab legs, though this is time-consuming. You now have strongly flavoured brown meat and delicate white meat, which can be eaten separately or together, according to the recipe.

CRAB SALAD

Season up the dark meat with salt and pepper, and maybe some nutmeg. Scatter the white meat on top, and serve with a crisp salad, dressed with olive oil and lemon juice. Serve one crab per person.

CRAB PASTA SAUCE

Make a tomato sauce to your usual recipe and to the quantities desired, seasoning it with a little fresh basil. Boil the pasta, drain and serve with the tomato sauce on top, adding white crab meat as you take it to table. A crisp salad with an olive oil and lemon dressing goes well with this, too. One crab should provide enough meat to flavour two or three portions of pasta sauce.

FI'S CRAB TARTLETS WITH OATMEAL PASTRY

For the filling:
200g mixed crab meat
1 large onion, chopped and softened in butter
2 tbsp crème fraiche
1 tbsp gin or other spirit
1 egg
Tabasco, salt and pepper

For the pastry:
115g plain flour
115g fine oatmeal (or porridge oats blitzed in a blender)
1 tsp salt
115g butter
1 egg

Set the onions to soften gently while you make the pastry. A food processor speeds the preparation, but you can rub the butter in by hand if you prefer. Stir in the egg once this is done, adding a drop of water if the mixture seems too dry and crumbly. Roll out fairly thinly, using non-stick parchment below and above it if it sticks. Cut out rounds for a patty-pan tray and place it in a preheated oven at 190°C for about 8 minutes, to half-cook the pastry.

Remove the pan with the onions from the heat and add the rest of the ingredients, except for the egg, seasoning cautiously and tasting a little, to get it right. Tabasco is good in moderation but could drown the crab flavour. Lastly stir in the egg to bind, and spoon the mixture into each of the little tarts. Return the tray to the oven and bake a further 10 minutes, or until the crab mixture has cooked through and is turning a delicate brown. Cool a little before serving, or store in the fridge and serve cold.

PARTAN PIE

Meg Dods, Sir Walter Scott's fictional cook in *St Ronan's Well* (1823) published 'her' *Cook and Housewife's Manual* in 1828. It contains a treasure trove of Scottish recipes, including this one for partan pie. 'Partan' is an old name for crab. Below is an adaptation with more reference to actual quantities than the original.

All the meat from one medium or large crab
2 tbsp cider vinegar
1 tbsp, heaped, butter
1 tbsp mustard
8 tbsp, heaped, brown breadcrumbs
Salt, pepper and nutmeg to taste

Heat the butter in a saucepan and stir in the vinegar, mustard and crab meat, adding the breadcrumbs last. Return the mixture to the cleaned crab shell and place under the grill until the surface has browned and the mixture is warmed through. A large crab will feed two in this way, especially if served with plenty of hot buttered toast, or oatcakes if you want to be very traditional.

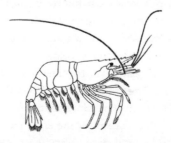

SHRIMPS AND PRAWNS

Although closely related and very similar in appearance, shrimps (*Crangonidae*) and prawns (*Palaemonidae*) inhabit different worlds.

Prawns of various species can be found in rock pools, where their lovely translucent bodies flit, ghost-like, dropping to the bottom where they feed. You seldom notice them to begin with, but sit quietly and you will see them speeding about. In Scottish rock pools they seldom seem to attain any great size, and it is difficult to catch them with a hand net as they can see you through the clear water. The old method, used when fishing off rocks into the edge of the sea, as well as in pools, was to use a baited drop net. Like all the maritime crustaceans, prawns are scavengers and will go for rotting baits.

It is possible to make a net using something like old net curtains but you can also source something called a 'crab drop net' on the Internet. Devise a method of keeping bait secured to its bottom: the old nets had two strings across the circumference, drawn tight so that bait could be inserted between them. Suspend the net with three strings that meet at a float half a metre above it, making one of them much longer, to be held on the shore. A hand line that you can buy from a fishing tackle shop is ideal. This too should have a float attached, in case you drop it in. Drop your net into your chosen pool, which should be a deep one, and let it lie for a few minutes. Haul the net in as smoothly and swiftly as you can and see what you have hopping around at the bottom. It may contain shore crabs rather than prawns, but people have been known to catch lobsters in drop nets. Beware their claws if you have such good fortune!

You might possibly catch other prawn-like creatures in a drop net, such as squat lobsters ('Squaddies') *Galathea spp*, or Dublin Bay prawns, *Nephrops norvegicus*, now more commonly known as langoustines. The former sometimes appear from under stones low down the tidal zone on the west coast. Without netting them from a boat, the latter are not likely to be present in sufficient numbers to be caught.

Brown shrimps, *Crangon spp*, and many other shrimps are sand dwellers. Traditional shrimping nets can still be ordered on the Internet. The net will have a stout wooden handle and a wooden half-moon frame. Across the diameter is fixed a strong board that tapers towards the front like a shovel. You wade into the rising tide on a sandy beach, pushing the blade of the net a few centimetres into the sand as you go, push-trawling in fact. At the end of a sweep you bring the net swiftly to the surface and look at your catch. You will soon know whether it's a good beach for shrimps, for if it is, there should be plenty flicking about inside. Store them in a deep pail of seawater until you have enough for a boiling.

I have fond childhood memories of taking shrimps home, washing them in fresh water, and then boiling them in salted water for a few minutes, until they turned pink (or pink with brown speckles if they are truly brown shrimps). If this seems cruel – and it is – pop a bag of shrimps into the freezer for an hour. This will almost certainly kill them, but more gently. Take them out and quickly place them in a pot of boiling salty water until they turn pink and curl up. They will be spoiled by over-cooking, and they're best eaten immediately. It's a good idea to make people prepare their own for eating, as it's very fiddly pulling off the heads and loosening the tail armour so that it slips away. The easiest way is to stretch the creature out, then press its head and tail end together before you try to pull them apart. It's worth the trouble, as they are truly delicious.

POTTED SHRIMPS

This is a real delicacy. It will take devotion to make it from the raw ingredients, as you will have to shell all the shrimps first.

> *2 cups shelled brown shrimps*
> *100g butter*
> *Mace, cayenne, nutmeg to taste*
> *A little additional butter for sealing*

Melt the butter gently in a pan with a blade of mace. Throw in the shrimps and a tiny pinch of cayenne and another of nutmeg. Taste to see whether you have enough spice. Stir until all the shrimps are coated, then decant into small ramekins. Cool, then melt another wedge of butter to pour over the tops to seal the pots. They will keep in the fridge for a couple of days at most.

SEA URCHINS

The grapefruit-sized, pink sea urchin, *Echinus esculentus*, is, as its Latin name suggests, edible. It's probably most familiar as a nearly spherical empty shell, found on the strandline after the animal has died. The living creatures can be found in rock pools, principally but not exclusively on the west coast. They have short, strong spines, and may appear covered with seaweed, presumably used as camouflage. Never popular as food here, sea urchins have been extensively harvested for the continental market. They are now considered too few to gather. Enjoy looking at them, but don't disturb them; instead, leave them to multiply.

MUSSELS
Mytilus edulis (feusgan)

The general word for shellfish in Gaelic is *maorach*, a word that can be seen in some coastal place-names such as Camas a' Mhaoraich, and may refer to mussels or other species of mollusc. Within memory shellfish have been an important resource, especially in the early spring, when the sheep were lean.

Mussels are commonly found attached to rocks or any structure that is regularly submerged, often among the holdfasts of large seaweeds. The rules about collecting from clean water apply very strongly to mussels, with another observation, that if they come from a gritty environment, they will be gritty to eat. Many of the mussels found on the west coast and on island beaches unfortunately fall into this category. If they take in sand and grit as they feed, they tend to retain it. Each particle is duly coated with mother of pearl (nacre) to make it less abrasive to the mussel's soft body. It's impossible to remove the tiny pearls before you eat, so you encounter them as an unpleasant crunch. One day, of course, you might come upon a large and beautiful pearl, but too many creatures would have to die before you found it. Turn your attention rather to finding an unpolluted, rocky shore, with no sand in the vicinity. There the mussels should be good to collect.

Preparing mussels for the pot

Cook mussels the same day that you collect them, discarding any with cracked shells and any that will not close when you give their shell a sharp tap. With really fresh mussels there should be almost none of these. Remove the beard-like strands of the creatures' attachment threads and scrub them under running water. Now they are ready for the pot.

MUSSEL STEW

Here is a Scots dish not unlike the classic *moules marinière* but with the addition of milk and cream.

50–60 mussels
2 onions, finely chopped and softened in a little butter
2 heaped tbsp butter and a little extra for the onion
2 heaped tbsp flour
½ bottle white wine
1 cup single cream
Parsley, salt and pepper to taste

Put a layer of mussels in a large saucepan and cover with wine. Bring to a simmer, shaking the pan frequently so that you can see when they open. At that point remove them to a dish and add another layer. Continue to do this until all the mussels have opened. Remove the mussels from their shells, pouring back into the original pan any extra liquor that runs out. Melt the butter in a different pan, stir in the flour, then add the mussel liquor bit by bit, stirring with a wire whisk to get rid of any lumps. Next add the milk and stir over gentle heat until the sauce thickens. Add the onion and bring the sauce back to a simmer. Finally, add the cream and the mussels, stir and reheat, but do not allow the mixture to boil or the mussels will toughen. Garnish with a good scatter of parsley and serve with plain boiled potatoes, as this is a rich dish. Other shellfish like cockles, whelks, winkles, and even limpets can be used in addition to, or as substitutes for, mussels.

MEG DODS' MUSSEL BROSE

Meg's method for preparing mussels for brose is much the same as for the stew in the previous recipe, but you omit the wine and introduce a fish stock. You can substitute vegetable stock if you don't have any.

Per person:
8 mussels (approx)
1 cup fish stock or milk and water
2 heaped tbsp medium oatmeal
Salt and pepper (unless the stock is already quite salty)

Put the mussels in a metal pan with a lid over moderate heat. Shake the pan, checking frequently to see when the mussels open, and removing them as they do to a warm dish. Reduce the heat if the liquor seems to be evaporating, or add a little water (you will be using all the resulting stock). Add the fish stock, or milk and water mixture, and bring to a simmer. Meanwhile toast the oatmeal, dry, in a large frying pan over moderate heat, shaking the pan constantly so that it browns just a little without scorching. This brings out the best of its nutty flavour. Once ready, put the oatmeal in a warmed soup bowl, place the mussels in the stock, and pour this mixture over the oatmeal, stirring quickly so as to form 'knots' rather than a solid lump. If it seems too solid, add a little boiling water. Serve immediately. This thick-textured dish is uniquely Scottish. You can, of course, make this for three or four people at once, providing you have all the ingredients and equipment, including the final soup bowls, lined up and ready, as the process is quite quick.

COCKLES, GAPER CLAMS AND RAZOR CLAMS

Cockles (*coilleag* or *srùban*) are familiar bivalves with corrugated, slightly irregular shells, common on some sandy shores, where they bury themselves about 6cm deep as the tide goes out. Remember that they, and the other small molluscs, are particularly likely to pick up pollutants from their environment, so carefully check the beach for sewage outflows. This will minimise the number of places cockles may be safely dug. Ask locally if you think you have found a place, and listen to advice about tides. In Morecambe Bay a few years ago, several cockle-gatherers who were taken there by a gangmaster were drowned by the rapid sweep of the incoming tide.

There is a further rule about cockle digging, and other clams. Dig neatly, with a small, pointed trowel rather than a large garden spade. Identify the breathing hole (gapers have two) of the clam and dig slightly to one side of it, to make sure it is large enough to collect. If it is small, leave it, refill your pit, and try again. These creatures live at a critical depth, and if more sand and mud is heaped over their breathing holes, they will die, and your excavations will damage more than the creatures you actually extract. So always refill excavations.

Gaper clams, such as the sand gaper, *Mya arenaria*, are grey, with ridged shells that do not close, so that the creature cannot fully retract inside. Razor shells, common razor, *Ensis ensis* (*muirsgian*), and pod razor, *Ensis siliqua*, or 'spoots' in the vernacular, are well known from the tideline. They are long, and shaped like old-fashioned cut-throat blades. Gapers prefer a mixture of sand and mud, and razor clams pure sand. Both are good to eat but razors are no longer common and should be preserved unless they are locally very abundant. Gapers live up to 20cm deep, and razors even deeper. The latter are hard to catch, as they can burrow very quickly and evade your trowel. That helps to ensure the future of the species, although commercial digging for razors may still go on in a few places. An alternative method is to sprinkle salt into the razor clam's breathing hole. This makes it extend its siphon to the surface where it can be grabbed and wheeched out. A friend recently dug half a dozen from a perfect site on the west, only to hear his nine-year-old say, "You said we should never take animals from the wild unless we really need them as food and Grannie has supper ready for us." He carefully put the razors back, right way up and at the depth he had found them, and went home to lamb stew.

If you do take a few of either of these clams to try, cook them following the cleaning and opening procedure described for mussels and cockles and let them simmer for 4 or 5 minutes. Beware of overcooking them as they go tough and leathery. Preserve their liquor to make a sauce, and eat them simply with wholemeal bread and butter, to savour their taste and texture. It should probably be a once-in-a-lifetime experience for razor clams, although gapers (*Myidae*) and carpet shells (*Veneridae*), another family of edible clams, may be common enough in some districts to make them more regular food.

COCKLES AND BAKED TATTIES

2 baking potatoes
1 litre of fresh cockles in their shells
1 large (or 2 smaller) onion/s, chopped
4 rashers streaky bacon, chopped
2 sticks celery, chopped
1 heaped tbsp butter
1 heaped tbsp flour
1 cup milk
Salt and pepper to taste

Scrub the potatoes and put them in a hot oven to bake (approximately 1 hour).

Prepare the cockles in a similar way to mussels, washing them, scrubbing them, and washing them again to remove the grit. Put a little water in a large pan and add a layer of cockles. Heat them for around 5 minutes, shaking the pan and removing them, as they open, to a warm colander over a dish to collect the liquor. Repeat until all are open. Fry the onion, celery (which can be omitted if you prefer), and bacon in butter until the first are soft and the other just starting to crisp. Stir in the flour and then add the liquor and milk, stirring with a wire whisk to remove lumps. Once the sauce has thickened, set it aside with a lid, adding a little more milk if it seems too solid. When the potatoes are ready, take from the oven and cut the top off each, removing some of the flesh. Add this chopped or mashed up to the sauce to make a thick mixture. Test the seasoning and adjust. It may not need any salt if the bacon has provided enough. Lastly add the mussels and spoon the mixture back into the potatoes. Sprinkle with grated parmesan or a Scottish cheese like Orkney or Dunlop, and return to the oven for a few minutes. Serve with a garnish of parsley.

WHELKS

In Scotland this term covers several species of snail-like molluscs that live on rocks. In the rest of the UK, the word refers to the common whelk, *Buccinum undatum*, or 'buckies'. These are large, white, spiralled creatures, whose shells are common on beaches. Although they are good to eat, buckies inhabit pools below the tideline, where they prey on other shellfish by boring through them to extract their soft bodies. You can seldom pick them from pools in the inter-tidal zone. That is not true of the smaller common periwinkle, *Littorina littorea* (*faochagan*), the type of 'whelk' most often found in Scotland. They are recognisable as compact brown or greenish snails with a distinctly pointed end to their spirals. They cling to rocks on most shores where they graze on algae and can be harvested in great numbers. Commercial gathering is not as common as it was 20 years ago when Scotland's beaches provided vast numbers for the national fish markets. Sacks of the animals were left for days in secure places below the tideline, waiting for a merchant's van to collect them. They can live for a long time out of water, so if you gather them, put a lid on any vessel you leave them in – otherwise you may find yourself rounding them up from remote corners where they have wandered in search of the returning tide.

Dog whelks, *Nucella lapillus*, are distinguished by their more tapered, ridged shells, usually grey or off-white, and a distinct channel in the shell mouth, which the siphon groove. They live in crevices on barnacle-encrusted rocks and, though not as common as periwinkles, are still easy to find. Unlike periwinkles, a dog whelk is a predator, using its radula (toothed tongue) to bore holes in other molluscs.

Great fun can be had by gathering whelks and cooking them on the shore. You will need a pot you can hang from an arrangement of driftwood, or robust enough to sit on stones, some cloths for handling hot shells, and a good number of long pins. Collect the whelks, enough for everyone to have a few to taste, and wash them to remove grit. This is best done in fresh water but seawater will do. Cook them in fresh water, however, or they will be overwhelmingly salty. Issue everyone with a cloth with a pin threaded through it. Make small children sit over a coat or similar surface so that you can retrieve the pins as they are dropped. Use the cloth to protect your fingers from the hot shell and the pin to winkle out the winkle and ponder on which meaning came first! Eat when still warm, spitting out the hard little operculum, or trap-door, of the shellfish. They make a good picnic food, served with brown bread and butter, with beer or cider to wash them down.

MEG DODS' WINKLE SOUP

This simple recipe was collected from the Hebrides by 'Meg' in the early 19th century. Hebrideans have continued to make use of the abundant crop of whelks and winkles to be found in rock pools right up until recent times.

1 small pail of winkles
1 litre unseasoned fish stock and/or milk and water
4 heaped tbsp medium oatmeal
Pepper to taste

Gather winkles from the rocks at low tide. Wash them, put them in a pot, cover with water and bring them to the boil. Simmer for just a couple of minutes, then strain the winkles, preserving their liquor. Remove each winkle from its shell using a long pin, and set aside in a warm dish. Strain the liquor through a fine sieve to remove any sand or grit. Add an equal quantity of fish stock (or water and milk), making sure that the resulting stock is not too salty. Dilute it with a little more milk if it is. Bring to a simmer and add the oatmeal in a continuous stream, stirring all the time with a spurtle or whisk, to avoid lumps. Stir until the meal cooks and the broth starts to thicken, which should take from 10 to 20 minutes, depending on the coarseness of the oatmeal. Finally, add the winkles and serve.

LIMPETS
Patella spp. (bàirnich)

These common molluscs are cone-shaped and usually white. You can find them adhering to rocks almost anywhere but their size and cone height depend on their location on the shore. They are edible but rubbery, so almost universally despised except as a famine food. Jane Cheape, in her book about food of the Scottish islands, reports that women from Jura would collect them, and also people from Swona, an island in the Pentland Firth that is now uninhabited. To gather them you have to surprise them by suddenly kicking them off their rock with a well-aimed blow from a stout boot. If you disturb one first, it will cling, well, like a limpet. Once you kick a limpet, it's done for, so persevere and remove with a stout bladed knife rather than kicking more. Go lightly because once the first kick is felt through the rock the rest will clamp down too. If you are winkle-picking and having a beach fire, try a few. The taste is good, but the texture hard to enjoy. The best use for limpets is as bait when crabbing but you can always throw a few into a shellfish stew, like the mussel one (on page 81). They will give your guests' jaws some exercise.

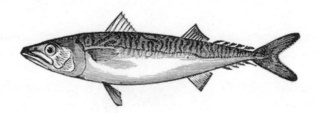

FISH

Fishing is a lifetime obsession for some. For those who just want to dabble when on holiday, a cheap hand-line, baited with a limpet, mussel, or bit of old fish – the sorts of things you can easily find on a beach – can be fun. Sometimes it will bring home the supper. Jetties make good fishing stations, as they as relatively safe, but rocky outcrops are also good. Children will need careful supervision. Saithe and pollack, *Pollachius spp*, seem to be the commonest catch off the west coast. Mackerel (*Scomber scombrus*) are common in some years from about July onwards, so you may find them during the summer holidays. They will take a glittering lure in preference to bait. Two other summer species that can be caught along the shores of estuaries are the flat fish dabs (*Limanda limanda*) and flounders (*Pleuronectidae*). They will take bait, including ragworm or lugworm.

Digging for bait

Sandy shores with a mixture of mud on the east coast used to be frequented by fishermen who walked them daily with a spade, looking for worm-casts. The lugworm (*Arenicola marina*) leaves a distinctive small hollow in the sand, with a coil of excreted sand and a small hole beside it. Ragworms (*Nereididae*) are discernible by the single hole they leave in wet sand or mud. Both species can burrow fast, so the bait-digger has to be swift and skilled. Worms can be stored in a box of wet sand for a day or two, but don't take more than you will need, and use them fast.

SEAWEED

It's reassuring to know that there do not seem to be any species of seaweed on our shores that are innately poisonous. That said, there are plenty that are tough and tasteless, so you have to put in some work to identify the best species for eating. Some of them are delicious and almost all of them are particularly nutritious. However, some words of caution are needed. Like shellfish, seaweeds for eating should never be gathered from polluted shores. Consult the SEPA list of safe bathing beaches and you will have some starting guidelines about where to gather. There are plenty of island and west coast shores that are clean enough, of course, but not listed by SEPA as they are not suitable for bathing because of other dangers. Use your powers of observation to see how far a site is from human habitation. If it's a long way from where folk live, it's probably a long way from industrial and domestic pollution. This matters, as the brown seaweeds in particular can accumulate heavy metals. If you are only eating them occasionally, this is no problem. However, if they become a regular part of your diet, you should be extra careful about their provenance.

Wherever you collect seaweed, rinse it well in clear sea water to get rid of sand and grit. To dry it, spread it on trays or racks in a warm, dry place and leave it for a few days, turning occasionally until it is really crisp. At this stage, crumble or chop it and dry for a few more days before storing in screw-top jars. In this form, seaweeds can be used as seasoning. For use as a vegetable, take fresh fronds, rinse them in fresh water, and follow the instructions given in recipes.

Bittersweet

Black medick

Bitter vetch

Kidney vetch

Wood vetch

Tufted vetch

Restharrow

Lousewort

Yellow rattle

Evening primrose

Viper's bugloss

Sea holly

Oyster plant

Single-flowered
wintergreen

Twinflower

Coralroot orchid

Sea centaury

Lady's bedstraw

Golden saxifrage

Marsh marigold

Corn marigold

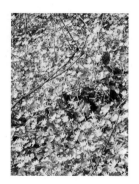

Celandine

Buttercup

Mountain avens

Sea mayweed

Ragged robin

Sheepsbit

Field gentian

Burnet rose

Downy rose

Eel grass

Sea thrift

Sea campion

Scottish primrose

Spring squill

Sea lavender

Sea sandwort

Sea milkwort

Sea aster

Sea purslane

Sea rocket

Early marsh orchid

Frog orchid

Greater
butterfly orchid

Flag iris

Wild thyme*

Sea kale

Alexanders

Scots lovage

Marsh samphire

Rock samphire

Scurvy grass

Orache

Sea buckthorn

*Unlike other species on this page, wild thyme is not for consumption.

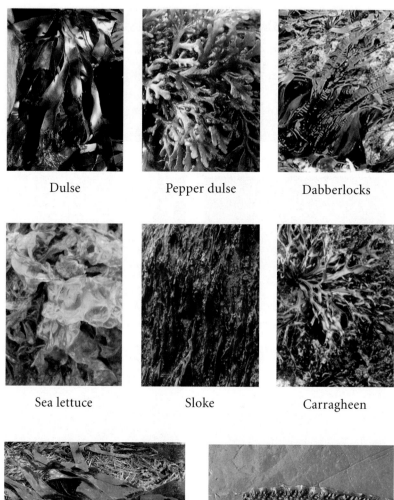

Dulse

Pepper dulse

Dabberlocks

Sea lettuce

Sloke

Carragheen

Oarweed

Sugar wrack

These photos are not sufficient for identification purposes. See recommended guides.

Velvet swimming crab

Edible crab

Squat lobster

Common spider crab

Cockles

Mussels

Common periwinkles

Limpets

Rocky beaches are best for seaweed. You can take fresh kelp from a sandy beach if it has blown in on a very recent storm, but it is better to pick the growing plants. Most species are common but one of the most delicious is less so, and should be harvested with regard to its long-term survival. Identification is made easier by the following site, which has better pictures than most books, many of them taken by divers. They show the weeds afloat. www.seaweed.ie.

Kelp: Tangleweed/Oarweed

KELP

Kelp is a rather general term which can apply to a range of seaweeds, most of them large, brown and leathery that tend to grow at and below low water. They are washed off rocks in high seas and great, thick carpets of them can be stranded on the shore, where they can be easily harvested as fertiliser. They were the mainstay of crofting agriculture on the coast and can contribute to garden fertility. They are high in phosphates rather than nitrogen, so need to be collected and spread before they decompose, otherwise their goodness will be lost. The following three are the most useful edible species of kelp.

KELP: TANGLEWEED OR OARWEED
Laminaria digitata (stamh)

This is a broad weed that originates from a single stem. Its wide blade splits about a third of the way up into a number of flat, finger-like fronds, making it look a little like a palm tree. Splitting is due to damage and in sheltered locations the splitting is much less. You will find it low in the inter-tidal zone, so it is best collected at low water. You will not need many specimens to give you a store of dried *kombu*, as the Japanese call it. It is not particularly interesting to eat by itself but is a good basis for a seaweed stock as it is high in sodium, potassium, certain amino acids and glutamic acids, and also in dietary fibre.

KELP: DABBERLOCKS
Alaria esculenta (mircean or gruaigean)

This is a beautiful, long, ribbon-like weed with slightly feathered edges and a pronounced central rib. It is usually brown but sometimes has a yellowy-green tinge. It can be more than 2m long and prefers deeper water, so only occurs at the very bottom of the tidal zone.

KELP: SUGAR WRACK
Sacchinaria latissima (langadal or ròc)

The light brown ruffled ribbons of sugar wrack are easy to find on the west and on rockier parts of the east coast. They are broad and dimpled, and not as thick as many kelps. The holdfast is shaped rather like a claw. Like many of these large kelps, sugar wrack grows in the lowest part of the tidal zone, so you need low water to find it. It has a rich, sweet taste and when roasted takes on an almost bacon-like flavour, making it a useful seasoning.

SEAWEED STOCK

Wash some lengths of oarweed or other kelp, chop and add to a pan with water to cover. Bring slowly to a simmer and cook for 20 minutes before removing the weed. Seaweeds other than kelp can be added for different flavours. Use in soups, stews and rice dishes like the one below.

SLOKE OR LAVER
Porphyra spp (slòcan)

This plant has lettuce-like leaves up to about 20cm long. They are olive green to dark purple but look black when exposed by the tide. Sloke lives higher up the shore than the kelp family and you can find it covering rocks and often attached to shellfish such as mussels. The thinness of the leafy fronds makes them collapse and adhere to surfaces so that it is difficult to make out individual plants. It is widely distributed and easy to find on most coasts. Even sandy shores usually provide some homes for sloke, which has a long history of use in Scotland. Traditionally it was boiled to a jelly. This can be stored for weeks and is highly nutritious, being high in protein, Vitamins C and B_{12}, and in anti-oxidants. The flavour is olive-like and good on oatcakes or toast. Sloke can also be eaten as a salad or lightly cooked. Both of these methods will preserve its Vitamin C content, which is reduced by long boiling.

SLOKE JELLY

Steep the washed seaweed in fresh water for an hour or two, then place it in a thick-bottomed pot with water to cover it. Cook gently for several hours, stirring very frequently, until it becomes a dark green jelly.

Use the jelly seasoned with pepper and lemon juice to accompany mutton or lamb.

SLOKAN

Marian McNeill gives this recipe from Barra in her book *The Scots Kitchen*: its name is clearly from the Gaelic.

Make the sloke jelly as in the recipe above.

> *'Put in a pan with a very little sea water. Make it hot, withdraw it, and beat well; heat it up, withdraw it, and beat again, and continue this process until it is reduced to a pulp. Do not let it cook. Add salt, pepper and a little butter. Serve hot, with mashed potatoes round it'.*

DULSE
Palminaria palmata (duileasg)

The flat, thin, divided blades of dulse, up to 30cm long, are highly variable in shape and arise from a disc-shaped holdfast, often with a short stem, or 'stipe' as it is called botanically. They are distinctly red-brown rather than purple, so can be distinguished from sloke which they otherwise resemble in some ways. They have slightly more texture, and do not collapse in the same way that sloke does when not in water.

Dulse is a valuable vegetable, full of iron. It can be eaten raw or cooked but is best dried (traditionally done over embers) and used as a snack or as seasoning. It has a smoky flavour. Dulse can be used like carragen, to make a milk jelly.

DULSE AS A VEGETABLE

Wash carefully and simmer until tender. Strain, cut into small pieces, add butter and seasoning and return to the pan. Serve when piping hot.

A SIMPLE SEAWEED SOUP

Sloke or dulse
Milk
Butter
Lemon juice
Pepper and salt

Wash the seaweeds thoroughly in fresh water, drain, then boil them gently in milk. Stir frequently, and use a potato masher or a spurtle to break up the fibres. The soup will thicken slowly and can be served when you think the consistency is right. It's best to strain the remains of the seaweed out of the soup, then season to taste. If it seems too bland, season at the last moment with dried, crumbled pepper dulse, which will add a fine flavour.

PEPPER DULSE
Osmundea pinnatifida

This is the truffle of the seaweed world, and even tastes a little like that sought-after mushroom. It is a small brown seaweed, varying from yellowy to deep brown, or even red-brown, according to how far down the tidal zone it is growing. Its fronds are flat and divided, each section ending in little lobed fingers, which are quite distinctive once you have learnt them. Pepper dulse attaches to the vertical face of rocks from the middle to the lower section of the shore. As it is not as common as many other weeds, harvest it carefully with scissors, taking only enough for your own needs. Leave plenty to regenerate, for pepper dulse is a real treasure of the sea.

Try pepper dulse raw or dry it, grind it and use it for seasoning fish. If you want to cook with the fresh weed, add it at the last moment of cooking or you may lose some of its flavour.

SEAWEED RICE OR BARLEY

1 large onion, chopped
1 large carrot, chopped finely
2 sticks celery, chopped finely
2 rashers of bacon (optional)
Olive oil
1 cup rice or pot barley
2 cups seaweed stock (or vegetable stock)
1 cup fresh pepper dulse, chopped finely

Soften the vegetables (not including the seaweed) in olive oil and stir in the rice or barley. Add all the stock, stirring until fully mixed. Cover and leave on a very low heat for 15 to 20 minutes for rice, or 30 to 40 minutes for barley. Once the rice or barley is soft, stir in the pepper dulse and serve.

CARRAGEEN
Chondrus crispus (cairgean)

Known as Irish moss, sea moss, or carrageen, this is probably the seaweed best known for culinary use. It is a red weed, of short (about 20cm), tree-like form with many cartilaginous branches. You can find it on many shores, from the mid to the lower tidal zone. It is rich in alginates and still used as an industrial source for making agar for scientific and other uses. Traditionally it is the thickener of milk puddings, which were called moulds, but are now more fashionably named after the similar Italian dish, panna cotta.

SEAWEED MOULD OR PANNA COTTA

A generous handful of carrageen
1 litre whole milk
Lemon zest from the rind of 1 lemon
1 tbsp castor sugar
1 large egg, optional (see below)
Whisky, vanilla essence or nutmeg for flavouring as desired

Wash the seaweed thoroughly and steep it for an hour or two, throwing away the water. If you want to remove the seaside tang, which can have a slightly fishy undertone, bring to the boil in half a litre of water, then strain off and discard the water. Heat the carrageen in the milk, adding the lemon zest. Bring slowly to the boil and keep barely simmering for a few minutes until it thickens. Stir in about a tablespoonful of sugar and stir. Beat the egg in a separate basin. Cool a little, strain off the seaweed, and pour the milk mixture over the beaten egg, stirring continuously. Return to the pan and reheat until almost boiling. Taste and add flavourings as desired. Pour into a mould to cool. Traditionally served with cream, this is quite a rich dish.

If you want to enjoy the traditional seaweed tang, omit the blanching and omit the egg, cooking the carrageen gently in the milk for at least 20 minutes before straining and cooling.

SEA LETTUCE
Ulva lactuca (glasag)

The broad folds of sea lettuce are easy to distinguish as the name describes it perfectly. The blades are thin and soft, appearing slightly translucent as they float from their disc-shaped hold-fasts in rock pools. Sea lettuce is common, particularly on shores where fresh water runs out to sea. A high level of nutrients favours the growth of sea lettuce, but too much nitrogen from agricultural run-off can kill whole beds of it. The resulting mass of weeds that floats on to beaches stinks as it decays, and the gases given off, particularly hydrogen sulphide, are toxic. So beware if the beach is bright green or slimy black and stinking!

Harvested fresh, sea lettuce can be washed and eaten raw. It's rich in iron and other minerals, Vitamins A, B_{12} and C, and also in protein. The taste is good and lends itself well to a French dressing. Dried, it makes a very useful and pretty seasoning for white fish. As the leaves are so thin, the drying process only takes a few hours in a warm environment, or even less in a low oven. Crumble the dried leaves and store in a jar.

SEAWEED SALAD

2 handfuls sea lettuce
1 handful of dulse, dabberlocks or sugar wrack, or a combination
½ handful pepper dulse, finely chopped
Lettuce, optional

Cut all the fresh, washed seaweeds into small sections. If you only have one variety, use shredded real lettuce to bulk out the salad. Dress with olive oil and lemon juice, with a little sugar added. The result is chewy but the flavour is interesting.

'INSTANT' SEAWEED BROTH

This takes two minutes but you will need your own stock of dried, chopped seaweeds, or else packets of prepared sea lettuce and dulse.

½ tsp vegetable stock powder
2 tbsp medium oatmeal
Generous scatter of dried seaweeds.

Add all the ingredients to your soup bowl. Boil a kettle and pour on a large cup of boiling water, stirring all the time. Adjust seasoning, adding pepper and possibly some more seaweed. The texture is slightly gritty for some tastes but the flavour is excellent.

EDIBLE
SEASIDE PLANTS

Many of the most palatable seaside plants are confined to south-west Scotland. Even there, sea kale, rock samphire, and sea beet are not abundant. Samphire, one of the most succulent species of estuarine shores also has a limited number of habitats. Silverweed is common but strictly speaking should not be dug up without a landowner's permission –an impossible condition on the seashore.

Gathering other seaside plants does not require landowner permission in Scotland. But collect them sparingly, with respect for the survival of individuals and of plant colonies, never stripping a single plant or taking more than you are sure you can use. The notes on different species will give you an idea of which plants are rare, and worthy of particular respect.

MARSH SAMPHIRE
Salicornia europaea

The short, fleshy branches of samphire, or glasswort, can be found along estuarine shores in a few places on the east coast of Scotland and a few more on the south-west. In some seasons it can be abundant in places like the Dornoch Firth, but commercial harvesting is threatening samphire. Any collecting should be extremely limited, as taking it kills the plant. Recognise it by its bright green (yellowing when old), knobbly, tubular branches ending in spikes. They carry only tiny pairs of leaflets and extremely wee flowers, making it hard to believe they are part of the spinach family.

Samphire is nutritious and tasty. Simply wash it thoroughly and boil it briefly. Eat with your fingers, pulling the tender flesh off the fibrous branches with your teeth.

Marsh samphire

ROCK SAMPHIRE
Crithmum maritimum

Not related to marsh samphire, this fleshy-leaved member of the carrot family can really be found only in the south-west of Scotland. The authors of *Flora Celtica* quote Murdo McNeill from the early 20th century as saying that it was much sought-after in Colonsay. It was traditionally boiled or pickled and has a resinous taste. This must surely be the samphire referred to in *King Lear* – in Act 4, Scene 6, Edgar calls gathering it a 'dreadful trade': as it grows on cliffs, collecting it must have been, and still could be, hazardous.

SCOTS LOVAGE
Ligusticum scoticum

A plant of dunes and cliffs, Scots lovage occurs in the north. It is a member of the *Umbellifera* (carrot) family, which immediately signals caution as several of that tribe are extremely toxic. If you have a good floral ID book and are sure of your identification of lovage, it makes a wonderful seasoning, particularly for soup. A small bunch, added towards the end of cooking, will impart a delightful, rich flavour and aroma to vegetable soup or Scots broth.

ALEXANDERS

Not common in Scotland, but you do see it round the Firth of Forth and on some of the islands in the Clyde. It is easy to identify as it is the only yellow-flowered *Umbellifera* (*see caution in lovage, above*) that has glossy, bright green leaves and black seeds. It's a handsome plant that makes a succulent vegetable when steamed and buttered. Its flavour is strong enough to use as the main ingredient in a rice or barley dish.

SEA KALE
Crambe maritima

A very attractive plant, with its grey, deeply indented, long, slightly frilly leaves, sea kale is not common on Scottish shores as the shingle it requires is not a common habitat. You can find it in a few coastal places in Dumfries and Galloway. It used to be a popular vegetable, but the uncooked leaves are tough to eat except when very young. If you want to taste it, it is best to buy from a grower such as Plants with Purpose. Blanch the growing shoots: they're delectable!

SEA BEET
Beta vulgaris spp. maritima

The glossy, fleshy leaves of sea beet resemble those of perpetual spinach and make attractive clumps on the upper levels of beaches and dunes in the few places where they abound in Scotland: notably the south-west and some parts of the Moray Firth. It is a good vegetable, especially when the leaves are young in early summer, but there is not enough of it in Scotland for the responsible forager to collect it in quantity. Confine yourself to sampling, and enjoy this richer and more robust form of spinach in a small helping.

SILVERWEED
Potentilla anserina

Silverweed is related to the strawberry, as you can see from the shape of its yellow flowers and its habit of sending out runners. Its distinctive pinnate leaves are dull green above and silver beneath. It is common on sandy shores, well up from the tideline. Long ago it was considered an invaluable resource, as the roots could be roasted and ground for meal, or else boiled and eaten directly. More recently it was known as a famine food. The leaves can be used as a vegetable: tiny ones are palatable chopped into a salad and bigger ones can be boiled. Since the plant must be dug up to enjoy the roots, seaside ones should be left alone. If you can harvest from your own land or a place where you can seek permission, do try the roots. They taste fine but are so small, like rat-tails, that it is humbling to know how significant a part of the diet they used to be in some parts of the Hebrides.

SCURVY GRASS
Cochlearia spp

Scurvy grass has small, bright green, nearly heart-shaped leaves that are fleshy like those of many maritime plants. Its small flowers have four white petals with four green bracts within, making a distinct little cross in the centre of each. It is common on coastal grassland in many areas of Scotland. This is a famine food; edible and very rich in Vitamin C, but bitter and not very palatable raw. If you take to their pungent flavour, which resembles horseradish, try eating them chopped with a good French dressing.

SEA BUCKTHORN
Hippophae rhamnoides

Native to south-eastern Britain but widely introduced in eastern Scotland to stabilise sand dunes, sea buckthorn is now so common as to be a pest along much of the East Lothian coast. It is a thorny shrub with narrow, silvery leaves and distinctive orange berries. These ripen late in the year and are best picked when frozen as they otherwise tend to squash into a gelatinous mush when pulled from the branch. Sea buckthorn berries are real winter treasure stores as they have exceptional nutritional qualities. They are very rich indeed in Vitamins C, E, B_1, B_2 and K, as well as in beneficial fatty acids, minerals, and anti-oxidants. The pulp from the astringent berries can be processed and used as a daily winter tonic, to flavour puddings, to make jellies, to flavour rich meats like game, or even as a substitute for vinegar in salad dressing. The flavour is complex and interesting, but not to everyone's taste.

SEA BUCKTHORN SORBET

4 cups sea buckthorn berries
Boiling water
1 cup sugar
1 cup cold water

Lightly process about a quarter of the berries in a blender. Pour in half a cup of boiling water and press the resulting slurry through a fine sieve, saving the juice. Repeat three times over with the remaining berries until you have at least two cups of juice. Place sugar and cold water in a pan and heat, stirring constantly until the sugar dissolves. Simmer for about five minutes to make a syrup. Leave to cool before adding the sea buckthorn pulp. At this stage, the mixture can be transferred to an ice cream maker. If your household lacks one, pour into an old ice cream box or similar container and place in the freezer until it starts to freeze. Remove, beat with an electric hand-held blender or mixer, and return to the freezer. Repeat this process at roughly half hour intervals until the sorbet is fully frozen. It's laborious but the result is excellent. You can make it from bottled pulp, which is sold in some wholefood stores.

LIST OF COMMON EDIBLE COASTAL PLANTS & SEAWEEDS

ENGLISH NAME	LATIN NAME	GAELIC NAME
Sea buckthorn	*Hippophae rhamnoides*	*ràmh-dhroigheann mara*
Sea kale	*Crambe maritime*	*càl na mara*
Alexanders	*Smyrnium olusatrum*	*lus nan gràn dubh*
Scots lovage	*Lingusticum scoticum*	*sunais*
Samphire or glasswort	*Salicornia europaea*	*lus na glainne*
Rock samphire	*Crithmum maritimum*	*saimbhir*
Scurvy grass	*Cochlearia officinalis*	
Orache	*Atriplex spp*	
Dulse	*Palmaria palmate*	*duileasg*
Pepper dulse	*Osmundea pinnatifida*	*duileasg piobarach*
Sloke	*Poprhyra spp*	*slòcan*
Dabberlocks	*Alaria esculenta*	*mircean*
Sea lettuce	*Ulva lactuca*	*glasag*
Sugar wrack	*Saccharina latissimi*	*langadal*
Tangle or oarweed	*Laminaria digitata*	*stamh*
Carragheen/ Irish Moss	*Chondrus crispus*	*cairgein*

These species are illustrated in the colour plates section. However, the photographs provided are by no means sufficient as a guide to identification. Always gather with someone who has expert knowledge and experience who knows the species beyond doubt, or else identify plants with the help of a guide and double-check with an experienced forager before consuming. Refer to the guides listed on page xx.

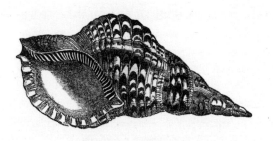

FORAGING FOR OTHER TREASURES

Who can return from a seaside walk without some trophy? Driftwood may be the thing for you, or pebbles, or for children it may simply be amassing shells or pieces of coloured sea glass for mosaics. Much will depend on the beach and what it naturally affords.

SEA SHELLS

Sandy beaches are the best place to find shells as they are usually smashed to pieces by the waves on rocky shores. Each beach will have its distinctive varieties. Some East Lothian ones major in large shells: oysters, big whelks and substantial razor shells. Others may have tiny bivalves like the butterfly shell, with its twin lobes as small and pink as a child's fingernail, and much loved and sought after by discerning children. The Coral Beaches on Skye not only abound in endless fragments of white coral but seem to have an extraordinary resource of very small shells. Amongst the tiny top shells, tower shells, minute mussels and small yellow periwinkles, you can occasionally find a compact little cowrie shell – *faoiteag* in Gaelic, and considered very lucky. Treasure indeed!

DRIFTWOOD

Driftwood is almost ubiquitous on beaches, although some Scottish ones are subject to scouring tides that tend to carry it away. To some, driftwood is just a usable resource, good for wood-stoves, though not for open fires as it spits. To others the manner in which the sea scours and shapes twigs, branches, or sections of cut wood is endlessly fascinating. A knobbly stick, worn smooth in places and with a knot suggesting an eye, will be pounced upon by the driftwood hunter: raw material for an animal sculpture, or simply something to hold and enjoy for the walk.

PEBBLES

The underlying geology mostly dictates the type of pebbles on a beach, but that is not always the whole story. Rivers wash rocks downstream, rounding and smoothing them in the process. Glaciers moved them in the past, and currents and storms can carry material for quite a distance. Below a sandstone cliff on the Moray Firth you might find granite pebbles, gleaming as the tide retreats, green, grey, red, or mottled. They may have originated in the Cairngorms or perhaps in Norway. Below sandstone rocks in Berwickshire, white spheres of quartz catch the eye, and sometimes blood-red pebbles of jasper. Particular shapes may be of interest: the near sphere was one summer's obsession for me. Stones with white lines of quartz, made fashionable by a postcard image some years ago, can also be quite magnetic, as can agates. If this all sounds very acquisitive, the scale of such collecting is always modest. The wholesale removal of pebbles by commercial interests is damaging to beaches but the quest for the perfect pocket stone will do no harm. The pleasure in turning over the stone in the pocket, and recalling the sea and sky of the day it was found, never fades.

BEACHCOMBING

The invention of plastic has changed beachcombing beyond recognition. It used to be said that if you had enough patience the sea would yield everything that you might need. That was in the days of willow creels, wooden fish boxes, hemp rope, natural nets, and lower expectations about need! Even then it wasn't quite true. The other flip-flop, pair to the one that fitted me, never did show up, nor did a piece of amber. Old fishermen on the east coast would regularly collect it after a storm, but they had the eye.

A day or two after a storm is still the best time to see what has washed up. Most cargoes are containerised but timber sometimes is not, and baulks occasionally float in. Small vessels lose equipment but you may not always want to take home the yellow oil skins you heave dripping from the beach, slimy and alive with sand-hoppers. Rope is often the very best find. Hemp is never found these days, but serviceable lengths of nylon rope, from thick twine to hawser, are almost always to be had.

As for plastic, it is a scourge. Every plastic item that has ever entered the sea is still there in some form, from battered boxes and endless bottles to the tiny 'nurdles' (beads of plastic used by industry) which the organisation Fidra is hoping to remove entirely from the Firth of Forth. Masses of items find their way into the water every day, leading to great burdens of rubbish on our beautiful beaches. The onus is on every one of us, not simply to refrain from littering, but to become active in clearing the mess. The Marine Conservation Society invites volunteers to sign up with their Beachwatch programme, so that efforts to clean up can be co-ordinated. Once a year, on the third weekend in September, they have Beachwatch Big Weekend, when tonnes of litter are picked up, bagged and taken away by volunteers. Any rubbish that will not readily decay – especially plastic, glass, nylon, fishing tackle (particularly damaging to wildlife), and metal – is better off in landfill than polluting the oceans. Never burn plastic on the beach or anywhere else as the result is highly toxic.

Marine Conservation Society: mcsuk.org
Fidra's The Great Nurdle Hunt: nurdlehunt.org.uk

ROCK POOLS

The miniature worlds of rock pools, with their brightly coloured plants and animals, are alluring for everyone, and children in particular. The palette of pinks, russets and mossy greens makes them wonderful subjects for photographs. If explored with due care for the state of the tide, slippery rocks and barnacles (the sharp-edged volcano-shaped shells that encrust many rocks), pools make an ideal place for initiating the young in the wonders of nature.

Coastal Bounty

Most rocky coasts, except where the bedrock wears smooth and offers few footholds to life, abound in pools. Some sandy coasts, like those of East Lothian, have some rocky areas with accessible pools. The lower down the intertidal zone, the richer they are likely to be.

Look for shore crabs, ranging from tiny 'pea crabs' to substantial green-backs; sea-anemones, red or orange jelly-blobs exposed by the tide that become swaying flower-like animals once immersed; stumpy fish like blennies; eel-like butterfish, with white-ringed black blobs along their upper side; sponges, which may appear as crater-covered mats, or as soft pipe-like forms; sea-mats, which coat rocks in bright pink, white, grey, or orangey-brown; the smaller sea weeds, such as Irish moss, with its broad reddish fronds, or cockscomb (*Plocamium*) with contrastingly delicate, coral-like red fronds; the many molluscs such as pyramid-shaped limpets, familiar mussels, pale snail-shaped dog whelks, or darker periwinkles, or topshells, which often show some mother-of-pearl amongst their pinks or greens. Amongst these snail-like creatures, look for hermit crabs, which scuttle along, using cast shells as mobile homes. Sea urchins, small green and spiny, or tennis-ball-sized and pink, are another marvel, as are their cousins, the brittle stars, which sometimes appear in large numbers in pools on the west coast. Related to them are the more common starfish, some varieties of which occur on sandy shores as well as rocky ones. Darting amongst all this more static life, you may see prawns, although, being translucent, they are hard to spot. Patient 'still-watching' pays dividends, and is a good discipline for everyone, not just the kids. Beware their big relatives, the edible crabs. These may be seen in pools near the low-tide mark, where they often lurk in cracks or under overhanging rocks. Never try to extract them with your hands as they can trap you by clamping their legs, and leave you to drown in the rising tide!

Some of these creatures can be captured for closer viewing. Use a light commercial net, or make your own with bamboo, an old coat-hanger, and some net curtain. A tupperware box, or clear plastic bucket, makes a good aquarium. Be sure to handle the creatures as gently as possible, and to put them back after a few minutes. Take a hand-lens with you to discover the small elements of the seashore and check out the Highland Seashore Biodiversity website for guided exploration days.

highlandbiodiversity.com/seashore.asp

The East Neuk coast generally has good pools, and stretches of the west coast and island coasts that have horizontal planes of rock, rather than steep vertical ones, make excellent hunting grounds. So be aware of rock formations and seek out pools, whether you are on the mainland, the west coast of Skye, the Ross of Mull, or somewhere with wonderful beaches, like Colonsay.

Fi Martynoga

FIVE

COASTAL
CULTURE

Ardnamurchan Point

The sea must be ice-cold, but it's like looking into a seething cauldron, its heaving waters on the brink of boiling over. Billowing up to meet our awestruck gaze, the waves jostle with quite unthinkable force: it's an arresting – and somehow powerfully unsettling – scene. For the duration of this moment, we take a vertiginous glimpse into the unknown, sense our real insignificance in the scheme of things. In the background, the dark expanse extends away towards an unseen horizon – just as intimidating as you'd expect the ocean deeps to be. Closer to us, though, the surface of the water seems transfigured, the sea suffused with an eerie radiance of white: there's something almost spiritual in the play of surge and sunlight here. Losing its distinction in long exposure, this seascape takes on the character of a painting – albeit of a particularly disturbing sort. Beautiful, but hardly pleasing, it assaults the viewer and takes the aesthetic sense by storm – pretty much the definition of the sublime.

No one could see 'The Swelling of the Sea' and seriously doubt that photography is an art. Nor, though, can they question the terrible majesty of nature, before which the most confident, accomplished artist can't help but quail. The picture was taken in 1990, by the Glasgow-based American photographer Thomas Joshua Cooper, off Ardnamurchan – hence, in the most literal, geographical sense, the work's subtitle, 'Furthest West', though this is surely a study too in human limitations. The sense that this is it, the point beyond which we cannot venture, is surely central to the imaginative excitement we experience at any of the extremities of the Scottish coast – from Cape Wrath or John o' Groats to the Mull of Galloway or Kintyre. Yet we feel something of the same when we find ourselves in any coastal setting. Whether we stand on a giddy and windswept cliff top, look out across a saltmarsh, scramble over rocks or stroll along a bare and sandy beach, there's a thrilling sense of being at the outer edge of things.

And yet there's a sense as well of edges dissolving, boundaries blurred as water laps up against land, and wave and spray meet mist and rain. Chronological frontiers can be transcended too: looking out from the farthest flung, most isolated headlands, we see so little sign of human habitation that we can feel that we're standing apart, outwith the flow of history.

Cape Wrath

Mystic places

In the rain-drenched island of Chiloé off the coast off Chile, local legend has it that everything on land has its counterpart below the sea. Hosts of exotic mythic beings inhabit the subaquatic world and have to be approached with care. Centuries of science and Presbyterianism have consigned the spirits of Scotland's coasts to the province of the fairytale and to a prized but patronised 'folk tradition'. Even now, however, there's a special magic to be felt. Wherever we are around the coast, whatever time of day or year and regardless of the weather, the sea is always making its presence felt. Whether it's crashing in on jagged rocks, racing across an open stretch of sand, retreating down a muddy estuary or lapping up against a harbour wall, the sea is doing something – bringing life and change to every scene. No one was ever an atheist in a foxhole, they say; by the same token, it's hard to watch waves breaking on rocks or pounding against a breakwater without feeling the faintest pagan stirrings at the power – and the perpetual animation – of the sea.

Boundary or bridge?

Strong as our psychological sense may be of the coast as some sort of terminus or limit, we should remember that this feeling is of comparatively recent date. Historically, coastal zones were regarded as a 'liminal' environment – in other words, as a threshold to be crossed in both directions. The sea was for many centuries as much a highway as a barrier. This was especially so where overland travel was restricted by the difficulty of the terrain, such as in Scotland (and, long before, in ancient Greece). Not so long ago, most land travel was slow and uncomfortable: as late as 1750, the coach from Edinburgh to London took twelve days. Well into the Industrial Age, the overland journey could seem too much like hard work. In John Galt's 1821 novel, *The Ayrshire Legatees*, Dr Pringle is summoned to London for a legal meeting, and he and his family decide to:

proceed by coach from Irvine to Greenock, there embark in a
steam-boat for Glasgow, and, crossing the country to Edinburgh,
take their passage at Leith in one of the smacks for London.

In the sixth century, the kingdom of Dál Riata took in the coast of western Scotland, from Arran and Argyll to Lochaber and Skye, as well as that of Antrim on the Ulster side. Such a state – a scattering of islands, peninsulas and coastal glens – makes absolutely no sense in modern terms. Back then, though, the North Channel was far less formidable a barrier than the rugged interiors on either side. The result was that it served as a sort of central plaza around which a disparate assemblage of land territories were grouped, turning our present-day perceptions inside out.

Clearly, a psycho-geography determined by maritime links like this must have felt very different from our own, though Dál Riata was by no means the last of these sea-spanning polities. The Viking voyages brought together coastal areas from Scandinavia to Scotland (and well beyond) into a single sphere in the 9th century. Shetland's Up Helly Aa fire festival may be one of those time-honoured Scottish traditions which date back only as far as Queen Victoria's reign, but the Norse inheritance it honours is real enough. Long after the raiding era was over, there were autonomous kingdoms under Viking-descended rulers in Orkney and Shetland, whilst the Kingdom of the Isles extended all the

High, low and wide

Culture … Few terms can have been more furiously contested: what is it, and what does it include? Music, fine art, literature, theatre … such things have been canonical in defining 'culture'. But how far should our definition really extend? In considering the cultural associations of Scotland's coasts, we might well think of Mendelssohn's overture, 'Fingal's Cave' – but should we also be thinking of 'Sunshine on Leith' (whether the song or film)? And, come to think of it, why would we stop there? From boatbuilding to ice cream, from architecture to the Arbroath Smokie, culture can come in myriad different forms.

'High' culture, as traditionally defined, certainly has its Scottish coastal connections. Think of Peter Maxwell Davies' music or the novels of George Mackay Brown. (Or, for that matter, think of The Martyrdom of St Magnus *(1977), a Peter Maxwell Davies opera based on a novel by George Mackay Brown.) Think of the Glasgow Boys – oddly named, in some ways, given that this group of painters set up a sort of artistic headquarters in Kirkcudbright. Or think of the Gaelic poetry of Raasay-born Sorley MacLean; Samuel Peploe's island seascapes; Compton Mackenzie's* Whisky Galore; *Dornoch Cathedral; Robert Louis Stevenson's 'Christmas at Sea'… the list of iconic coastal creations is by no means short. But this chapter takes a much wider view. 'Culture' here encompasses not only popular 'folk' traditions but also more general aspects of traditional lifestyles, work and crafts. Some of the subjects covered here (fishing; the textile trade; industrial glassmaking; steamships) might seem to belong more to economic or technological history, but they've all had their cultural implications for the way of life round Scotland's coasts.*

way from the Outer Hebrides to the Isle of Man. Not until the end of the 15th century was this separate state absorbed into Scotland, when Lord John Macdonald II surrendered his sovereignty to James IV. Even as the modern era approached, Scotland must have maintained this more ambiguous attitude to the sea and to its coasts to some extent. Growing English dominance can only have heightened the importance of an identity which transcended Britain. Looking outward – to France through the 'Auld Alliance'; to northern Europe through the Baltic trade – Scotland saw the North Sea as its connection with the Continent.

Coastal castles

This liminality is exemplified by Scotland's splendid coastal castles – like Dunnottar, south of Stonehaven; St Andrews, Fife; Sutherland's Keiss; Caerlaverock, near Dumfries. Eilean Donan Castle, standing on its little island where Loch Duich, Loch Long and Loch Alsh meet, was briefly captured by the Spanish in 1719, though the invaders quickly found themselves under siege by the Royal Navy. For the most part, though, far from making the country a fortress, these castles actually facilitated commerce,

Dunstaffnage Castle

Tantallon Castle (after Alexander Naysmith's painting)

guarding harbour approaches and inshore sea lanes. In their turn they were protected by the waters above which they stood.

In more modern times, as monuments, these structures have been assimilated into our sense of 'landscape', a dramatic aspect of the Scottish scene. From this perspective, they are as appealing – if not more so – when they're ruined. They have provided an important subject for artists since the taste for the gothic and sublime developed in the 18th century. Brought into the spotlight by Sir Walter Scott, who in 1806 had made it a major setting for his poetic epic *Marmion*, East Lothian's Tantallon Castle was memorably painted by Alexander Nasmyth.

Tradition. . . interrupted

The earliest finds from the Paleolithic period (that is the pre-agrarian Old Stone Age) in Scotland have predominantly been made close to coasts. This is not surprising given the additional dimension the sea and its resources would have afforded to nomadic communities pursuing a hunter-gathering lifestyle. Even with the advent of agriculture in the Neolithic period, the produce of the sea couldn't be dispensed with. A 'shell

Harvesting the seashore

Necessity was the mother of invention in some of Scotland's most marginal environments. Seaweed was widely gathered and eaten.

Dulse (page 94) is known to have been something of a staple for the monastic community on Iona – fried up with butter or stewed with oats.

Other species like sloke and carrageen were also harvested, though seaweed was generally stigmatised as a food for famine times. In times of comparative plenty it was more frequently used as a fertilizer, rich as it was in nitrogen and potassium. Typically, it was buried in 'lazy beds' – basically, composted plots for growing root vegetables – though it could also be simply scattered onto open fields. New applications emerged in modern times: kelp became an important source of soda and potash for the glass industry from the 18th century; iodine for pharmaceuticals was extracted from seaweed from the 19th.

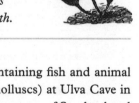

midden' (basically a rubbish heap containing fish and animal bones as well as the shells of edible molluscs) at Ulva Cave in Mull is one of several found around the coasts of Scotland and has been dated to as early as 7650 BCE.

Land and sea were brought together too in the 'traditional' Scottish lifestyle of crofting – essentially a farming/fishing hybrid. It's easy to imagine that this is a regime which has come down unbroken from prehistoric times. In fact, this pattern of life seems to have developed in the aftermath of the Highland Clearances in the 18th and 19th centuries. Dislodged from richer lands in the interior, communities settled along the coasts where they were more or less forced to supplement their agricultural activities with fishing.

And, in many cases, by fowling – young men abseiling hundreds of feet down sheer cliffs to take the eggs of puffins, guillemots, razorbills, kittiwakes, fulmars and other seabirds (see St Kilda, page 172). Or, as on the uninhabited Sula Sgeir rock, to collect young guga or gannet fledglings by the thousand for their meat. Carried out by men from Lewis – some forty miles to the south – the guga hunt on Sula Sgeir continues to this day, though it's caused increasing controversy in recent years. In earlier times, seabirds were boiled down for their oil, which was used for lighting; or a string might simply be inserted through the throat of a dead storm petrel and pushed through the body where it could then be lit to make a sort of lamp.

Net product

Over the centuries, Scottish economic life moved from a subsistence model to a much more complex and specialised system. By the high medieval period, a significant herring fishery had emerged in the Firth of Forth and Clyde. Boats and drift nets were used as a supplementary activity became an industry in its own right.

Peterhead was probably the first important centre for fishing on the east coast. It began expanding from the 16th century, and by the end of the 18th century, the herring fishery was receiving encouragement from the government, given that its fleet was invaluable in turning out skilled and experienced recruits for the Royal Navy. Inducements were offered to shipbuilders and prices were guaranteed for fishermen. The early 19th century saw the emergence of Wick as a major fishing port followed by Fraserburgh and the harbours of Fife's East Neuk.

Two-masted, straight-keeled and cut off square at stem and stern, the first 'fifies' appeared in the 1850s. These sailing drifters had quite a turn of speed – important in getting a catch swiftly back to port where it would be processed by fishwives. Women worked in teams of three: two to cut and gut and one to pack the prepared fish in an ice-barrel.

The Isle of Colonsay *(image courtesy of www.colonsayestate.co.uk)*

Loch Leven, a fjord, looking toward the Ardnamurchan Peninsula

The Old Man of Hoy (above, left); Ailsa Craig from Girvan beach (right)
(photographs this page ©Ronald Turnbull)

Needle's Eye, Southerness, on the Solway Coast *(©Ronald Turnbull)*

Folded greywacke west of Pettico Wick, St Abbs Head *(©Ronald Turnbull)*

Gannet (© *Andreas Tripte*)

Puffin *(© Richard Bartz)*

Eider duck *(© Steve Garvie)*

Basking shark *(© Greg Skomal)*

Grey seal pup *(© Andreas Tripte)*

Arctic tern *(© Malene Thyssen)*

The Ring of Brodgar, Orkney *(© Steve Keiretsue)*

Dunnottar Castle, Aberdeenshire *(© Macieklew)*

Tobermory, Isle of Mull *(© Colin/Wikimedia Commons)*

Crail Harbour, Fife *(© S. Hunt)*

The lighthouse at Buchan Ness, near Boddam *(© Mkonikkara)*

Winter sun backlights the V&A and *RSS Discovery*, Dundee *(© S. Hunt)*

Helmsdale, c.1811: an important herring port

On the west coast Tobermory and Ullapool had both been founded earlier, in 1788 – specifically as fishing ports. Ullapool had been laid out by the famous engineer Thomas Telford. Fish was cured in salt for sale to the colonies and shipped out on a massive scale. The West Indies, Russia and the Baltic countries were all important markets for the Scottish fishery during the 19th century.

The fishery kept expanding: by the 1880s, over 7,000 ships and boats were involved. Steam drifters were introduced in 1900. Not just the boats but their winding-gear were powered so nets could be hauled in with a new ease, enhancing speed and, consequently, freshness. In the second half of the 20th century, however, this important industry pretty much imploded. Today no more than a few dozen ships (drifters and deep-sea trawlers) are still based around Scottish coast – though these are capable of catching as much as the early 20th-century fleet did on their own. Hence the importance of quotas in protecting precious stocks. The whole story is told in the Scottish Fisheries Museum in Anstruther (see page 186).

Creetown, near Kirkudbright

From Lady Nairn's 'Caller Herrin' (1845)

Wha'll buy my caller herrin
They're bonnie fish and halesome farin,
Wha'll buy my caller herrin,
New drawn frae the Forth.
When ye were sleepin on your pillows,
Dream'd ye aught o our puir fellows,
Darkling as they faced the billows,
Aa to fill the woven willows!

O when the creel o herrin passes
Ladies clad in silk and laces,
Gather in their braw pelisses,
Cast their heads and screw their faces…

Wha'll buy my caller herrin,
They're no brought here without brave darin,
Buy my caller herrin,
Ye little ken their worth.

There is still peril on the sea. It seems that no amount of modern technology can take the danger out of fishing. Lady Nairn is right: the catch is "no brought here without brave darin'". Kirkcudbright in particular has suffered two grave losses in recent decades. The trawler *Mhari-L* was lost in 1985 with all 15 crewmen – commemorated by Charlie Easterfield's monument of 1994. But this beautiful wooden statue, showing a mother and daughter anxiously awaiting a boat's return, has also had to be the memorial to the scallop-dredger, the *Solway Harvester*, which was lost in 2000 with seven men aboard.

The king of fish

Salmon was long considered the most prestigious of fish: Haaf netting is still used in the Solway. Standing waist-high in the water, the fisher holds up a broad rectangular-framed net at right angles to the current. The lower section can be detached and allowed to float free, enveloping the salmon when it swims in. This Scandinavian method was brought to Britain by the Vikings. Fixed stake nets are also used in the Solway Firth.

Smoked salmon as we know it is something of a parvenu taste in Britain, introduced towards the end of the 19th century by East European Jewish immigrants to London's East End. But salmon was 'kippered' on the Tweed from as early as the 13th century and other fish have been smoked for centuries in Scotland, generally after pre-curing in brine. Mallaig and Stornoway have both been famed for their kippers (smoked herring); north-east Scotland's Finnan Haddie is an essential ingredient in Cullen skink – a thick fish soup; haddock are also used for Arbroath smokies.

Whaling

Cetaceans have been hunted from the earliest times. The traditional method was to harpoon them, or – for big whales – corral them in the shallows with a crowd of boats and then drive them steadily inshore until they beached. As an industry, whaling took off in earnest in the middle of the 18th century. The main centre was Dundee, but other east coast ports played their part as well. Whalebone was the mainstay of the corset trade, whilst oil from whales was long used for lighting – and in jute manufacture, one of the other chief industries of Dundee. Steam-powered ships were introduced as early as the 1850s, but steel construction was resisted right to the end (which came just before the First World War). Wood-built vessels offered greater flexibility in pack ice.

Long hours of idleness at sea were passed by many whalers in the pursuit of scrimshaw – the often elaborate carving and engraving of whalebone, sperm-whale teeth or walrus tusks. The Scottish Fisheries Museum at Anstruther (see page 186) has some fine examples.

Whaling was not for the faint-hearted

Seals and selkies

The seal has long been hunted for its meat; its skin was traditionally used for making sporrans, giving the animal a special place in Scottish culture. Its importance – and the ease with which, watching gravely, head raised above the waterline, it can be anthropomorphised – are perhaps reflected in the stories told of selkies. These strange mythic creatures take the shape of seals for their lives at sea but can come ashore and cast their skins to assume a beautiful male or female human form. Stories abound of male selkies seducing vulnerable women (often women whose human

men have been taken by the sea), though there are tales too of men stealing female selkies' sealskins so that they are forced to remain ashore with them as their wives. The end again underlines the lim-character of the coastal environment as a threshold which can crossed in both directions.

Commerce and culture

Many of the east coast fishing harbours doubled as ports for trade: for example, Pittenweem exported the produce of Sir John Anstruther's coal mines and salt pans in the 1770s. But there had been a busy trade across the North Sea as far back as medieval times. Above all, raw wool was exchanged for finished textiles, but a wide variety of other products was shipped back and forth. Various agreements governed a commerce which was long dominated by the 'Staple' trade with the Low Countries: first through Bruges; later through Middleburg and Veere. There was a great deal of trade between Scotland and France as well, reflecting the 'Auld Alliance' between both kingdoms, and with the Hanseatic

The Scottish Traditional Boat Festival

Held every summer at Portsoy, Aberdeenshire, the STBF brings together Scottish boats of every sort from rowing skiffs to trawlers. There are races and exhibitions of art, photography and crafts – not just of the maritime kind, but of knitting and other skills. There are also old-style music and dancing displays and the chance to try traditional local food and drink, but the stars of the show are invariably the boats themselves.

ports, especially Danzig. And, of course, with England, at a time when land-transport was still difficult and slow.

The maritime trade, at least to begin with, was extremely local in its character: there were a great many small ports and no real economies to be had in scale. (The Pier House Museum at Symbister, on Whalsay in the Shetland Islands, gives a sense of the prosperity that could be enjoyed by a truly tiny port.) The nature of the trade changed over time, however, and from around the 15th century, larger ports like Leith were growing in importance. Timber, iron and luxuries from oranges to wine were all brought in through Scottish ports. There were sizeable Scottish communities in Poland in the 17th century and a brisk traffic in goods across the North Sea.

This traffic was not just in commodities but in ideas, difficult as it may be to pin these down in retrospect. They are to be found in concrete form, though, in the Dutch-influenced architecture to be seen at Crail, Culross and Dunbar, and also in Lamb's House, Leith – essentially a Hanseatic merchant's house in Scotland.

A puff for the Puffer

Scotland's seaborne trade was not reserved for these external markets only. Much internal commerce also took place by sea. This was always necessary given the number of island communities and the relative inaccessibility of even many mainland villages. To some extent it remains the case today. For centuries, then, there has been a brisk traffic back and forth between the west coast of Scotland and its offshore islands. The 1900s was no different in this regard, except that it was at this time (1905–23) that Neil Munro first brought the steamboat known as the 'Clyde Puffer' into the limelight with his comic tales of Para Handy (Peter Macfarlane) and his little ship, *The Vital Spark*.

The Puffers really were vital in keeping isolated communities supplied with everything from coal and candles to livestock and luxuries. Travellers and tourists could be taken too. These steamboats could go just about everywhere amongst the islands; they didn't even need wharves or harbours to load and unload since, with their flat bottoms, they could be beached between high tides.

Lost at sea

Shipwrecks have been an inevitable by-product of the fishing and shipping industries. It's estimated that there are in the region of 7,500 all told around the coasts of Scotland. Each of these is in its way as much a historical monument as any ruined monastery or castle: many are visited in this spirit by sub-aqua enthusiasts.

Some of these wrecks were simply working vessels which found themselves in the wrong place at the wrong time, with tragic consequences. Others had parts to play in the great dramas of history. In 1588, for example, several ships of the Spanish Armada were wrecked round the coast of Scotland after storms in the English Channel forced them to take the long way home. One such vessel was discovered off Kinlochbervie, north-west Sutherland, in 2002, whilst the *San Juan de Sicilia* is said to lie at the bottom of Tobermory harbour. A Dutch vessel was lost off Mingary Castle during the Covenanter War of the 1640s. Meanwhile, one of Cromwell's warships – wrecked off Duart Point, Mull, in 1653 – became a lasting memorial to Scotland's part in England's Civil War. A few decades later, in 1690, *HMS Dartmouth* sank in the Sound of Mull in the course of a mission to recruit the Clan MacLean to the Williamite cause.

Off Marwick Head, on the north-western side of Orkney's Mainland, is the spot where *HMS Hampshire* went down in 1916 with Herbert 'Your Country Needs You', the First Earl Kitchener, on board. Three years later, and just a few miles to the south-east, Germany's defeated fleet was deliberately scuttled by its crews in Scapa Flow: no fewer than 52 vessels were sunk in all. Most have since been salvaged and scrapped, but seven remain, preserved as monuments.

Lighting the way

It seems unlikely that seafaring will ever be entirely free of danger – plenty of vessels have been lost in modern times. But, given the number of hazards around its coasts and the importance of the shipping trade to the life of the nation, Scotland had to help lead the way when it came to preventive measures. Whilst the first modern lighthouse is generally considered to be the one built by John Smeaton on the Eddystone Rock in the English Channel (1759), Scotland didn't follow far behind. Kinnaird Head, Fraserburgh, the first lighthouse actually to be built on the Scottish mainland (1787), is now home to the Museum of Scottish Lighthouses. Actually a converted castle, some of its original character was retained when it was modified as a fortress against the elements – a guardian of seaborne trade.

The building of the Bell Rock Lighthouse, off the Angus coast, by Robert Stevenson and his men (1807–10), was an epic engineering achievement. The finished light – the first to be built on a partially-submerged rock foundation – was visited by its architect's young nephew, Robert Louis Stevenson, who contributed a little poem to the lighthouse log. A majestic sight and a stirring symbol of human endeavour in the face of a hostile nature, the lighthouse was famously painted by J.M.W. Turner in 1819. Stevenson was also responsible for the Mull of Galloway Lighthouse (1830), dramatically situated at Scotland's southernmost point. His son Alan designed the lighthouse on Skerryvore, southwest of Tiree: standing 48m (157ft), its tower

Navigation by rote

Iain Tharmoid Uilleam MacLeod, nicknamed 'Soolivan', was born on the Isle of Lewis in 1889. His recollections of a long and eventful life were brought together in a book by Calum Ferguson in 2004. His inimitable style makes him a perfect example of the Hebridean tradition of storytelling – but in other ways too he showed the strengths of the islands' oral culture. During a couple of spells in prison – first in the United States and then after that in Mexico – he would pass the time by reciting the Gaelic 'Duan a' Claidach' ('Shore Recital'). This was literally a list of all the headlands and gullies along the coast around his home – well over a hundred had to be given in exact order. An island party piece, it was mastered as a sort of memory game, yet many a fisherman would owe his life to what he had learned.

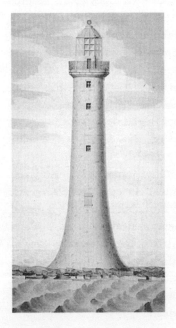

is Scotland's tallest. Its construction, like that of the Bell Rock Light, was an arduous and often dangerous labour: it took almost six years, from 1838 to 1844.

The romantic appeal of the lighthouse as an image is obvious, but it took on a darker undertone in 1900. It was then that all three keepers were found abruptly to have disappeared from the lighthouse on the Flannan Isles, west of Lewis. It's assumed that they were swept away together by a sudden wave, but the episode remains a mystery.

Cultural fabric

The importance of the cottage industry in textiles to the Hebrideans (using wool from local sheep) is recorded in the Statistical Account of Scotland published at the end of the 18th century. It was already an old tradition then, though the packaging and promotion of this cloth as 'Harris Tweed' is a modern phenomenon dating only from the 1840s. Catherine Murray, Countess of Dunmore, saw the possibilities for the cloth produced by local weavers on her Harris estate – especially those who were able to combine the traditional skills they'd gained in spinning, weaving and colouring with natural dyes with periods of training in the modern factories of the Lowlands. The fabric they produced was not only comfortable and hard-wearing, it was also beautifully patterned and coloured, with a distinctive 'outdoors' look. The countess took charge of organising and training the island's weavers and marketing the cloth they made as 'Harris Tweed'.

Home knitting was another centuries-old tradition which was commercialised in the 1850s with the opening of an agency in Edinburgh. The elaborately-patterned 'Fair Isle sweater' received a major boost from the patronage of the Prince of Wales (and future Edward VIII) in the 1920s, but this was just one of a wide range of attractive island knitwear. The industry endured a long and seemingly irreversible decline through the 20th century but is now enjoying something of a revival thanks to the vogue for hand-made prestige items.

The crockery coast

From the middle of the 18th century, the high-grade industrial manufacture of ceramics was taking place in coastal and port towns like Greenock, Bo'ness, Alloa, Kirkcaldy and along the south shore of the Forth. Not only could raw materials be readily brought in by sea, finished products could be shipped out again with ease. Again, the industry endured a long decline through the 20th century, but recent decades have seen a growth in artisan production in places like Fife's East Neuk.

Alloa also became a centre for the manufacture of glass in the 18th century, but the Scottish glass industry is believed to have been established much earlier by George Hay in 1610. Having secured a licence from James VI, he set up a workshop in 'Glass Cave' on the coast at Wemyss, Fife. Later he built factories at Leith and Prestonpans. In *The Industries of Scotland* (1869), David Bremner reported that 2,000 Scots were employed in glass-making. Bottle factories in Leith, Greenock and elsewhere served distilleries and breweries. More recently, the glass industry has returned to its roots with an expansion in artisan production.

Greenock in the 19th century: thriving port for freight and ferries

Artists' colonies

'Higher' up the creative cultural scale we move from artisanship to art. Scotland's coasts have always appealed to painters for their heart-stopping beauty and their peace. That said, it hasn't necessarily been the most sublimely scenic places that proved the most alluring: what Honfleur was to the French Impressionists, Kirkcudbright was to the Glasgow Boys (and Girls). Painters like E.A. Hornel, George Henry and Jessie M. King came to Kirkcudbright and established themselves there; other artists and collectors followed. Picturesque, rather than beautiful, it might be felt – but satisfyingly down-to-earth as well: a working town. This little fishing port is associated with the Scottish Colourists as well. Francis Cadell and Samuel Peploe both came to Kirkcudbright to work, though they also favoured other locations like Iona, North Berwick and the coast of Fife. There, both Pittenweem and Crail were home to artists' colonies in the late 19th century. Leslie Hunter loved to paint at Lower Largo.

Wigtown's status as Scotland's 'Book Town' dates back only to 1998 and was completely contrived as a way of regenerating a community hit hard by the collapse of local industries. But why knock it if it works? Wigtown is a paradise for the hardcore browser. The nearest thing it has to a serious literary association is with *Wigtown Ploughman* (1939) by John McNeillie (Ian Niall), but that novel's rediscovery has been well overdue. Peculiar as it is in its blend of rural idyll and social realism, it's a beautifully written book which makes compelling reading.

Beside the seaside

The Industrial Revolution was attended by a revolution in leisure. The urban working class was not just (to some extent) moneyed but mobile too. Yet whilst the great seaside resorts of England (such as Brighton, Blackpool and Southend) found their originating impetus in the coming of the railway, it was the steamboat that opened up resorts around the Firth of Clyde. The paddle-steamer crossing from Greenock or Gourock to Dunoon or Helensburgh,

The Royal and Ancient Golf Club of St Andrews in 1895

over to Arran or Kintyre or around the coast to Largs became an essential element in a Glaswegian Great Day Out.

On the east coast, as in England, the railway set the pace. Kinghorn, Fife, found its vocation as a resort after the opening of the Forth Bridge. As in England, too, there was a caste system amongst the coastal resorts. For Edinbourgeois trippers, North Berwick stood in much the same relation to Portobello as Lancashire's Lytham St Annes or Southport did to Blackpool. But Portobello certainly knew how to have fun, offering the Great British Seaside Experience in its totality: fish suppers, smutty postcards, saunters down the pier and prom, sandcastles, ice cream and donkey rides (and see page 186 for 'Porty' today).

More upmarket downtime was to be had at specialised golf resorts – most famously St Andrews on the coast of Fife. The 'Royal and Ancient' club had been 'Royal' since 1834 at which time it had already been established for 80 years. The game of golf itself was originally Scottish and had a strong connection with the coast, having first been played on 'Linksland', the scabby open areas between sand dunes. Some of the world's most illustrious courses are still to be found around the Scottish coast: like East Lothian's Muirfield, Gullane, or Ayrshire's Turnberry and Troon.

The 20th century saw a slow and seemingly inexorable decline in the fortunes of the Scottish Seaside, whose golden age had arguably been over even before 1900. Those resorts which have survived have generally done so by doubling as dormitory towns for the big cities, or by reinventing themselves in other ways – as centres for water sports, for instance. Times have changed, and – for better or for worse – we don't get quite the rush we once did from jostling our way down the promenade with an ice-cream cone or fighting for a deckchair on a crowded beach. Now we're individualists, bent on living to the full and stretching ourselves: we want to sail, surf, kayak, go cliff-climbing or coasteering. Even the least physically intrepid of us want at least to be adventurous in our consumer habits: Helensburgh hosts an annual Real Ale Festival and there's a Food Festival at Crail.

'Summer' fun

Music festivals

Specialism, it seems, is the way to go: every pastime catered for; every interest accommodated. Nowhere is this more clear than in the explosion in the number of music festivals around Scotland's coasts in recent years. Folk music is well to the fore, of course: it makes sense for traditional music to be played in something like its ancient setting and against the sort of stunning scenic backdrop afforded by the Isle of Mull Music Festival or the Barrafest. But why should the beards-and-Fair-Isle-sweaters brigade have all the fun? The Isle of Bute has a well-established Jazz Festival (and another for Linedance!); for lovers of classical chamber music there's always Islay's Cantilena.

From relaxation to renewal

Going out, I found, was really going in, wrote John Muir (1838–1914), Dunbar-born Sage of the Sierras, one of the fathers of the environmental movement in the United States, whose writing on wilderness environments profoundly influenced the conservation movement. His view is enthusiastically endorsed by Clare Cooper Marcus, Berkeley's Professor Emerita of Landscape Architecture, who became convinced that the sense of wonder we experience in the world's wild places opens up the heart to healing.

With time on her hands after her retirement and an attack of cancer to come to terms with, Marcus had the perfect chance to put these convictions to the test. And where better than in the peace and beauty of a sacred Scottish isle? Finding in that natural environment time and space for reflection, recollection and readjustment, she wrote a meditative memoir, *Iona Dreaming: The Healing Power of Place* (2010). Marcus' New Age way with Iona's ancient wisdom won't be everyone's cup of camomile infusion, but her courage and integrity still come shining through. As does the basic power of her premise: that, for whatever reason, being 'close to nature' can uplift.

All, or mostly, in the mind? Maybe. Not so much pathetic fallacy as scenic placebo? Perhaps. Yet few of us can fail to be stirred by the special atmosphere found along a lonely stretch of coast. And it's not just the natural beauty of the place: we're back where we started out this chapter with that mystic sense of liminality, that vague awareness of other dimensions, other possibilities, to be found at the threshold where land, sea and sky all meet. This, surely, must help explain the sacred associations of so many Scottish coastal places. Christianity, it's long been believed, was actually brought to Scotland by sea, by St Ninian, who landed on the southern coast of Galloway in the early fifth century. His chapel, on the windswept headland at Whithorn, could hardly be more underwhelming architecturally: it's little more than a ruined, roofless stone-built box. But the atmosphere here – as it is at the cave the saint is said to have made his hermitage, just around the coast – is thrilling in its spiritual resonance.

Iona itself has of course been a place of spiritual rebirth and prayer since St Columba's arrival with 13 fellow monks in 563 CE. Reputedly the burial place of the apostle, St Andrews Cathedral attracted pilgrims from far and wide across Europe in the centuries before the Reformation. It's hard to imagine that its setting – high up on a coastal cliff – didn't enhance its spiritual appeal.

Iona Abbey, with Mull in the background

What Columba and co were to the first millennium, New-Age activists may prove to be to the third. They have certainly found inspiration in beautiful spots around Scotland's coasts. The Findhorn Foundation Community had its origins in a caravan park outside the village of Findhorn, near Inverness, where Peter and Eileen Caddy came to live here with their children and their Canadian friend, Dorothy MacLean. In the decades since, the community has grown not just in size but also in (for want of a better word) respectability. The community's early interest in meditation and psychic communication, self-exploration and the occult went hand in hand with what then seemed equally eccentric enthusiasms for organic gardening and sustainable energy. In an age of growing green awareness, these last concerns seem much more mainstream: Findhorn has won UN approval for its pioneering work as an 'ecovillage'.

Puirt-a-beul

The ceilidh has come to be a popular gathering across the length and breadth of modern Scotland, though the case might be made that its deepest roots lie in the Gaelic west. The traditional tunes and dances are familiar to all. Altogether more recherché – *though its roots are shared – is the tradition of* puirt-a-beul *or 'mouth music', a sort of ancient Celtic scat-singing most closely associated with the Hebrides. If these cheerful songs have words at all, they're liable to be comic – not to say nonsensical. As often as not, they're strings of sounds which have no meaning.*

There seems to have been some overlap between the more festive puirt-a-beul *and the sort of rhythmic work songs sung by islanders to keep time and stave off boredom while waulking tweed. Tedious and demanding, this involved teams of people pounding out the dirt and grease from freshly woven cloth with their feet to cleanse and thicken it and make it softer.*

Marine Protected Areas

*Scotland has a network of areas designed to protect and enhance
its diverse coastal and marine ecosystems. The vast majority of its
231 sites are for nature conservation. They share the designations
given to land-based sites such as Special Areas of Conservation
(SAC) Special Protection Areas (SPA) and Sites of Special
Scientific Interest (SSSI). Many habitats, from rocky shores and
sea caves to deep sea coral and seaweed gardens, are protected to
the benefit of seabirds, plants, mammals and other fauna.*

*Eight areas are designated for their historical interest. They
are wrecks, dating from the 17th to the 20th centuries, from
Kinlochbervie to the Outer Skerries. The designation is intended
to save them from being ransacked by unofficial divers.*

*A site around Fair Isle is set aside for research. There, full
ecosystem protection benefits all sea life. Seabirds breed because
populations of sand eel and other prey fish are flourishing.
Careful monitoring is recording how this has a knock-on effect
for other fish, with view to developing a research programme into
local fisheries. It is hoped that a more general understanding of
how to create a sustainable fishing industry will ensue.*

*Several further areas are currently being considered for
MPA status, mostly to protect certain species. There's a Marine
Protected Areas map on the Scottish Government website, which
keeps track of policy developments in fishing and protection.*

Coastal costs

As yesterday's flaky, whole-earth hippie-ism becomes the hard-
nosed economic policy of today, could Scotland's coasts be key to
a golden eco-future? Hopes have been high for the impact which
might be made by wave power and tidal energy: one projected
scheme in the Pentland Firth could supply half of Scotland's elec-
tricity needs, it's claimed. Yet if, as many critics now fear, such
schemes prove as destructive to the coastal environment as the oil

industry already has, can this really be a price worth paying? It's become a truism to observe that the very 'wildest' of Scotland's inland landscapes has actually been very much the work of man. Countless centuries of woodcutting, grazing, cultivation – and, more recently, the Highland Clearances – have left their mark on even the most seemingly solitary of scenes. In between all the cities, towns, fishing villages and holiday developments, all the ports and harbours, wharves and marinas, long sections of the Scottish coasts remain substantially unspoiled. This is the closest we're going to get to the Scotland that has always been.

But even this hasn't been permanently fixed. 'Raised beaches' along the western coast of Jura, formed since the end of the Pleistocene period, are a reminder of how far things can change even regardless of human agency. Standing high above the current shoreline, these shingle terraces testify to the extent of 'glacio-isostatic uplift' – literally, the rising up of the earth's surface as warmer climates came and the crushing weight of the ice sheet was removed.

If Scotland's coastal environment is compromised by rising sea-levels in the century ahead of us, we'll have nobody to blame but ourselves, of course. It's a measure of our achievement as a species – though a deeply sobering one – that we've apparently been capable of effecting such change in climate. Great care is going to be needed in the coming times, but, whatever the long-term benefits of renewable energy, it's already clear that gung-ho green-ism can do immense damage of its own.

Can we look to culture to save Scotland's coasts? It doesn't seem likely on the evidence of history – not only from this country but around the world. Yet the more we can learn to treasure the cultural inheritance we have around our coasts, the more we enjoy the amenities it offers, the more likely we are to appreciate the need to give our coasts such protection as we can.

Michael Kerrigan

SIX

SCOTLAND'S
ISLANDS

*An 18th-century map
of the Western Isles*

The Admiralty Chart for the West Coast of Scotland gives an immediate overview of the archipelagos lying out from the mainland coasts. If you took a reel of cotton thread and tried to trace the coastline of each island, of the Inner and Outer Hebrides, you would be there for a long time. As a coastguard, I studied these shorelines most working days but it was still impossible to keep the contrasts and details, the havens and anchorages, surfers' shores and dangerous reefs clear in mind. Place names, of both Gaelic and Norse origin and anglicised Gaelic transliterations of Viking names, add still more complexity. Then there is the huge range of geology.

THE INNER
MACHAIR

Inner Hebrides and Small Isles
Isle of Mull

Much of the range of landscapes occurs on one island – Isle of Mull. It offers coastal exploration which is easy to access, so this varied territory will be a main focus of this biased sampling of island coasts. There are three short ferry crossings from the mainland to Mull but we'll start our approach from the perspective of the generations of mariners who navigated the Celtic sea road. Our historic trading havens in Cornwall, Wales, Isle of Man and across in Ireland are long left astern.

The pagodas of Islay and the Paps of Jura are history to us now. We have left the craggy Garvellachs or 'rough islands', west of Lunga. They say that the remains of the mother of Colum Chille (St Columba) still lie in this tide-swept group. Before we make landfall on the great landmass of Mull, look to Lismore, which lies to your right, in the mouth of Loch Linnhe. The shores are rocky but there is land that is still farmed. This change of terrain hosts a huge variety of sea and land birds.

A depth of fertile soil sufficient to sustain life is scarce in both the Inner and Outer Hebrides. That might explain why the stewardship of Lismore was contested by two saints, Colum Chille

Illustration from Robert Louis Stevenson's Kidnapped

and Moluig. To resolve the issue they decided that whoever put a finger on the island first would take jurisdiction. The monks used similar vessels, currachs, or wickerwork boats made of skin stretched over a light skeleton of timbers. It was close but Colum Chille was inching ahead. It was then that Moluig put his hand on the timber thwart and took the ship's axe to his own finger. He threw the severed digit well and it touched the shore before the rival vessel did. Lismore was now the territory of Moluig.

You will get a good view of Lady's Rock, off the southern tip of Lismore, from the Oban–Mull ferry. The name come from a later myth linked to clan feuds and a lingering ship of the Spanish Armada. The ferry docks in Craignure and if you stop off to view Duart Castle, perched on the headland just south of the ferry-port, you can hear the full story – or at least a version of it.

Many visitors proceed straight from the ferry to the western side of Mull. If you are under your own steam, I'd stop off at Carsaig Bay on the way. There is a steep, twisting track down to a boulder beach and stone pier. From there you can walk, with care, the coastal track all the way to Ardalanish point. You look out to the surge and spray that usually hints of the Torran Rocks. These wrecked many real ships, as well as the imaginary barque in Robert Louis Stevenson's *Kidnapped*.

Fionnphort, in the Ross of Mull (the southern peninsula that extends west), is the departure point for the small ferry that crosses the Sound of Iona. If you intend to cross over, it is well worth taking time to explore the mainland coast of the Ross of Mull first. The white sands of Erraid (www.erraid.com) stretch further as the tide ebbs. This is where Stevenson's David Balfour thinks the natives cruel as they laugh at his fate, stranded and shipwrecked. He does not realise that he can walk to the mainland when the tide falls. Of course you have still to check your times of high and low water.

In contrast to the intertwined lines of Celtic crosses, the elegant buildings of the Northern Lighthouse Board seek order and beauty in a spare and functional aesthetic. Erraid was the service station for the great granite lighthouse situated on the exposed rock of Dubh Artach, some 15 miles to the south-west of the Ross of Mull. Stevenson's father and uncles continued the family traditions of innovative engineering and Dubh Artach was one of their masterpieces, in service still. At one time the Northern Lighthouse Board was a steady employer of island men. They moved with their families from station to station all round the Scottish coasts. Some years ago, aboard a powerful lobster-boat which was working out of the Ross, I was taken under the lee of the high grey tower with its conspicuous red band. The deckhand told me his

Dubh Artach Light under construction

father served on Dubh Artach. Now the son was taking his share of the highest-quality lobsters which breed among the reefs, accessible only to the well-equipped and brave. These lobsters, which have indigo-coloured armour with flashes of International Orange, were cared for diligently after being hauled. Most of these, like the dived-for scallops and the creel-caught langoustines which are also targeted by bustling creel-boats all around Mull, went on refrigerated trucks direct to Spain.

These days the local restaurants and hotels have discovered that their guests are discriminating and want to taste local produce, perhaps none more so than the Ninth Wave restaurant in Fionnphort, which has produced its own book of recipes and lore (*Ninth Wave*, Birlinn, Edinburgh 2014). I met John Lamont when he was fishing velvet crab and he now sources shellfish and other local produce to be expertly presented by his Canadian wife, Carla.

The shoreline of the Ross makes fine walking. You can step on the pink granite, the thrift and thyme, and look to the 'Bull Hole' anchorage across from Iona where small creelers and the smaller pleasure yachts might shelter.

Accommodation is limited on Iona but it is well worth staying over. There is a good bunkhouse as well as a hotel and a few B&Bs. Even in summer, the island falls peaceful after the last evening ferry. The restoration work on the grey abbey, set in green, is impressive. As always it is the burial ground which provides hints of past lives, glories and tragedies. No fewer than 48 former kings of Scotland share this patch with the earls and chiefs of Ireland, Scandinavia and France. The man who inspired the MacBeth legend is one of them.

Whether you have any faith or not, you gain a sense of a trade in ideas as well as searches for settlements along this tideway. The influence of voyaging monks can be seen in carved stones and inked manuscripts. In the same way, Viking culture has left its trace in the design of the seaworthy vessels and functioning watermills of the Hebrides as well as in place names. Sadly, to see the great illuminated manuscripts, you have to make a wide detour to Trinity College, Dublin, where they are displayed in rotation.

Scotland's Islands

Staffa, a wildlife-watcher's paradise

Iona Abbey can be busy. Perhaps the best way to gain a sense of the monastic history is to walk out on the sandy shores or the close-grazed hills. You can imagine a place where periods of tranquillity were achieved despite the feuds and raids and ruthless politics of medieval Hebridean life.

Back on the mainland, some of the boats that take visitors to outlying islands have been adapted from fishing boat designs and are built from Scottish larch. These boats ply the same trade and the same route which took composer Felix Mendelssohn to Fingal's Cave, where he was inspired to create the concert overture, *The Hebrides* (also known as 'Fingal's Cave'). One company (Alternative Boat Charters, Iona) even offers the possibility of making the voyage under sail. I saw the blackish basalt cliffs of Staffa through a half gale on a heaving small crabber but, in good weather, visitors are taken right into the sea-cavern. There are recordings of echoing tin whistles. You may recognise basalt columns if you have seen them on the Antrim Coast and you may see them again on the Shiant Islands in the North Minch (the strait separating the Inner Hebrides and north-west Highlands from the Outer Hebrides). You get a sense of eruptions which might have happened only a day or two before your visit. A fault line of re-formed basalt runs between the pink and green granite. Iona had its quarry as well as the mainland but these are now also relics of lost engineering.

'Mula Insula' in the Blaeus' 1654 Atlas of Scotland

The landscape works of the Scottish Colourists were driven by the intensity of hues in rocks, sea and skies of this area. The shades as well as the shapes can be recognised. Samuel Peploe and Francis Cadell returned many times to attempt to capture some of the impossible range of colours which appear in the fast-changing light.

The low-lying island farm of Inch Kenneth is more difficult to reach. You may have to be content with walking the mainland shoreline shared by a broad community of wading species. The tall shape of a once-fine arts and crafts house juts up from the island. I have been lucky enough to make the crossing in a shallow-drafted boat after which we were greeted with iced coffee by the caretakers. Our tour took in the period furnishings, which hint at the astonishing story of the Mitford family who once owned the island. One daughter worshipped Hitler and another thought that Marx's words, as interpreted by Lenin and Stalin, were the blueprint for the future.

Outside there is evidence of older histories. Some of the carved stones in the old cemetery are as interesting as those at Iona. It seems that this was a burial ground which could be reached by a more sheltered crossing, if the winds prevented the transit to Iona. Even the dead can be storm-bound in the Hebrides.

Proceeding north, Ben More (listed as a Munro, a mountain over 3,000ft) dominates to landward. Look seaward and the shapes of another turf-topped volcanic archipelago reveals itself. Lunga, often likened to a dark battleship shape, was inhabited until the mid to late 19th century. But it is the shape of Bac Mòr, 'The Dutchman's Cap', which makes this group so distinct. Again, you may reach these islands by charter-boat. Most common seabird species can be sighted but puffins and Manx shearwater nest here in great numbers.

Ulva is another farming island. Its pastures used to host an unlikely herd of Jersey cows because the current owner liked cream on her strawberries. Ruined 'blackhouses' and run-rigs overrun with bracken tell of a ghost community and of the days before the emigrant ships anchored briefly here.

As well as the well-marked beaches of pale sand, like Calgary and Langamull (near the village of Dervaig and connected by road across to the north end of Mull), you might find pockets of sand amongst the boulders. It's well worth walking these shores (with caution in a westerly gale) as you gain a sense of continual change. The same beach can be unrecognisable after a single storm. It's also well worth dipping your wellington in the sand; you might stir cockles or even find a few native oysters. Both these species have been devastated by commercial gathering but they cling on to exposed shores where only a handful or two are taken for a supper. You need an exceptional range of tide to gather a few razorfish. They are tricky to extract from deep burrows but can still be gathered in areas where they have not been commercially exploited *(see the Coastal Bounty chapter)*.

There is bare moorland, pockets of farmed parks and swathes of close-planted conifers before you find the shoreline to the Sound of Mull on the east side of the island. After the herb-topped granite of the west side, the walk out from the bright painted harbour area of Tobermory is a complete contrast. You can spot woodland birds as well as seabirds on the path as you walk through scrub oak and birch. In season, the white clustered stars of wild garlic and an abundance of blue harebells side the route. It all opens out before a squat lighthouse building. From here you get a sense of a seagate where the bay opens out to the north and west. You might see cruising yachts, bound for the Small Isles or Skye, following much the same route Neil Gunn steered in his unreliable motor-launch just before the Second World War.

Vessels of bruised steel, of dulling plastic and of larch bright-work, lean against the stone pier to dry out. Fortunes were made by ring-netters hunting herring and by dredgers and divers looking for scallops. Now the wiser local hunters target langoustines, near to lobster in size, which are individually tubed and exported. Happily, local traders have seen the opportunity and you can now buy your share, uncooked or well-served, in the local outlets. I always gain a sense of civilisation here in 'Tob' with its excellent combined arts centre and recording studio, now linked to the innovative Mull Theatre company as Cromar Arts.

When you look out to Ardnamurchan Point (located on the most westerly headland of the Scottish mainland, and site of another major lighthouse), you gain a sense of wide open territories. Arguably the Inner Hebrides and the Ardnamurchan peninsula have a much weaker indigenous culture than the more distant Outer Hebrides. This can result in an interesting range of backgrounds and skills within the new communities and most islanders are happy to see a resident population holding on, wherever people come from. It has not always been like this as there have been times when people born locally have not been able to compete in the housing market with outsiders with more money.

Ardnamurchan Lighthouse

Coll and Tiree

Did you hear about the fellow from Tiree who landed on Mull and saw trees for the first time? "How do you get the potatoes to grow to that size?" he asked. Or so I was told by a native of Gometra, only a stepping stone out from Mull. But Coll and Tiree are the islands that seem to be 'under the waves'. I drew a sketch-map of the islands from a fishing boat north-west of Mull once and the skipper said, 'A flat line will do for Coll.' All this is good banter but dismisses the unique quality of walking Coll's open shores.

Tiree is now the territory of many communities. There are fleets of camper vans, often homes to surfers or windsurfers. The sudden shallowing of its shore can result in steep waves. There is also a higher incidence of sunshine here than in most parts of Scotland and a temperature modified by the last gasps of the Gulf Stream. At Scarinish harbour there is an exemplary modern timber-clad building – an appropriate boatshed for a community that still values sailing skills. There is room for modern dinghies and yachts but Tiree Annual Regatta, dating back to 1911, is really for the open boats flying extravagant tall dipping-lug sails. Weather permitting, the regatta is still scheduled for the first week in August.

Coastal life is celebrated in a unique way on this island with An Turas (Gaelic for 'a journey'), which is a 'building' that might be said to exist for its own sake. Situated at the Scarinish dockside, An Turas is ostensibly a shelter for the queue to the ferry, but in reality is a building where 'purpose' comes a long way down the list of priorities. Tunnel-shaped and made of different materials, An Turas is completed by the glass box at its end, exposing a panoramic sea view.

Already on this small island, with a current population of around 650, I have described two significant pieces of coastal architecture but that's nowhere near all. A third is part of the lasting legacy of the Northern Lighthouse Board and the Stevenson family. The Old Signal Tower at Hynish has been converted by the Hebridean Trust into a museum to celebrate Skerryvore Lighthouse. (The house which Robert Louis Stevenson occupied for a time in Bournemouth was called 'Skerryvore', after this lighthouse, his uncle Alan's solution to another offshore challenge.) Like the station at Erraid, the Lighthouse Board housing was built to a very high standard for its time and has proved enduring.

Also enduring, though built from neither brick nor stone nor mortar, are the folk tales linked to this geography. The Rev J.G. Campbell of Tiree (1836–91) was one of the early collectors. His retellings of traditions linked to a wandering character, MacPhee, are still told as hair-raising accounts of the supernatural. He corresponded with J.F. Campbell (Islay), another enlightened researcher, who transcribed what he heard with as little intervention as possible.

Another fable linked with Tiree is more pious. A tale from South Uist (still mainly Roman Catholic, in terms of majority religion, as in most of the chain of islands to the south of Benbecula) sketches the fate of a priest at the time of the Reformation. When so-called 'papist' icons were being destroyed, a priest was seized for trying to defend the buildings and relics of his faith. As no one dared put a blade to him, he was cast adrift in a tiny craft which washed up on the shores of Tiree. A poor crofter carried the surviving priest home and revived him with water and thin gruel. The priest told the man who had saved him that he might be persecuted himself for harbouring an outcast. When he heard that, the crofter led the priest through the house to his own father, who was on his deathbed. He was still of the old faith and thus he was given the comfort of the last rites.

Most visitors come here for the open outlooks west. The density of birds is immense and the waves are hypnotic, shag-green to male mallard green. Lobster indigo to peely-wally Baltic blue. To the north-east there is the narrow and challenging Gunna Sound, site of more than one shipwreck over the years. Another low island stretches out from here. If, like me, you have not yet made a landfall on Coll you might get a sense of the place from the illustrations of Mairi Hedderwick in the lively *Katie Morag* series of children's books. The artist lived here for some years. The TV versions of the books were filmed on Lewis, for practical reasons. There is hotel and quality bunkhouse accommodation but most people come here for the shore-walks, the outlooks to the higher Small Isles and to Skye, and for the myriad of birds.

Only three hours by ferry from Oban, it is worth walking these coasts in winter as well as summer, with an eye on the forecast and the avoidance of tight travel connections. The Coll section of the RSPB website suggests that during the darkest and coldest months you'll encounter the wintering barnacle, white-fronted and greylag geese, along with lapwings, curlews, golden plovers and long-tailed ducks and divers.

Muck, Rum, Eigg and Canna

The group of 'Small Isles' can be reached by the Caledonian MacBrayne Ferries running out of Mallaig but also by a seasonal passenger ferry normally running from Arisaig.

There is an excellent chance of a whale sighting en route. Minke whales are the most common species but several others are possible. Rum was chosen as the first site for the re-introduction of sea eagles. Their descendents now have a good claw-hold on both the Inner and Outer Hebrides. The scale of their wingspans ('barn-doors in the sky') and the brightness of their white tail against their dark belly and wings, make them easy to distinguish from the smaller golden eagle which you may also sight. Perhaps their story is not so different from the history of human settlement in these islands. Populations have been decimated and sometimes renewed.

Monastic settlement linked to Iona gave way to Norse settlement. Crofting peoples suffered the raids of Viking pirates but also from marauding rival clans from other islands (Mull as well as Skye and Harris). The terrible story of the massacre of the entire population of Eigg in a wide cave with a narrow mouth is told in many versions. Even more tragic are the accounts of the savage treatment of islanders by the officers and crews of the Royal Navy ships sent to tame the Highlands and Islands after the disastrous 1745 Jacobite Rebellion. It did not stop there. There is the all too familiar history of starvation and emigration. And in the case of Rum and Eigg there are instances of a more recent history of insensitive landlords.

The population of Eigg was virtually at war with the former British bobsleigh Olympic team member and laird of Eigg, Keith Schellenberg, who would drive around the island in his Rolls Royce. The car became a casualty of the war and Mr Schellenberg eventually admitted defeat, although the island passed to another inadequate landlord before being purchased by Isle of Eigg Heritage Trust. There is a happier history in neighbouring Canna. The collectors and analysts of folklore John Lorne Campbell and Margaret Fay Shaw worked from their island base to record songs and stories throughout the Outer Hebrides as well as the Inner. Fay Shaw's thorough approach informs her *Folksongs and Folklore of South Uist*. This definitive study is illustrated with her own strong photographs. John Lorne Campbell's use of tape-recorders was at the forefront of modern recording, and he transcribed the accounts with as little alteration as possible. In 1981, when the couple left Canna to the National Trust (buildings, farmland and all) they included an invaluable library as part of their gift. Fay Shaw lived on to the age of 101.

Muck now has its well-cared for farm. Eigg is in community ownership, pioneering many forms of sustainable living. Rum is accessible again and good quality accommodation can meet the needs of walkers on a budget. It used to be reached only by those who came to rent rooms in the big house and stalk deer.

The character of these members of 'The Small Isles' varies, from the farmland and sandy shores of Muck, to the bare high Cuillin ridge of Rum. It is like a smaller scale reflection of the

Black Cuillin ridge of Skye to the north but no less impressive when you look upwards from sea level from the anchorage of Loch Scresort. Eigg has its croftland on the lower slopes and the most recognisable shape of all the Scottish islands – the spur, or *sgurr*, of rock. Canna has a natural harbour. It is mainly farmland and its former prosperity is hinted at in the restrained but still impressive architecture of the surviving round tower from its

Episcopalian church. You can cross to Sanday by footbridge to see the islands guarding a lagoon, now a popular anchorage with the possibility of visitors' moorings and a café ashore. Other architectural remains range from An Coroghan to the east, which probably incorporates layers of historic fortification, to signs of monastic buildings, indicating Canna's role as a satellite of Iona Abbey.

The community buy-out of Eigg has led to a diverse, renewed community. Their enterprises have provided facilities for visitors as well as examples of sustainable development which might be taken up elsewhere. Arts projects have included residencies in a newly invented bothy. Perhaps parallels with Eigg can be found in the way the renewed community of Fair Isle (lying between Orkney and Shetland) includes those who work at timeless occupations in textiles, fishing and farming and those who have come to find new enterprises. But neither the survivors of the indigenous population nor the new pioneers would see these outlying islands as utopias.

Lucy Conway, a resident of Eigg, took part in the Cape Farewell group's Scottish Islands project, placing artists and scientists together on joint explorations to draw attention to evidence of climate change. She reminded the group that initiatives in researching sustainable ways of living should be seen as research rather than as a proven alternative way. Her own carbon footprint had to include a number of winter journeys with only one or two passengers aboard the scheduled ferry service.

And really that's what makes Scottish island life different from Scottish mainland life: the necessity of travel by sea or air to get home. The further out you are, the greater the difference. Now arguably Skye, with its bridge spanning the territory described by Gavin Maxwell, no longer has that characteristic, though Raasay and Rona do. The whole of Skye has a population of about 10,000 and a great body of its own literature and music. The outlook to the Cuillin across the Sound of Raasay echoes through much of the poetry of Sorley MacLean. He evokes the lost human habitations and cultivations on Raasay.

The main university campus building at Sabhal Mòr Ostaig, on Skye's Sleat Peninsula, is one of the few I know which seems to be orientated so that its strongest aspect can be seen from seaward. A sculpture in bronze by Will Maclean and Arthur Watson, set in its grounds, celebrates the sound sense of skeletal structure, essential to the culture of boatbuilding. The coastal walking close to the college is easier than most of Skye's challenging territory. The more rugged walks and climbs are well documented and numerous outdoor pursuits websites describe the routes in more detail than this sweeping survey can.

But since we're still under the shadow of the Black Cuillin, and since we're not going to make landfall this trip at the shore of Loch Scavaig, let us leave Skye with a sense of an open vista to the west. I was on the Glenelg ferry one day – that's the one which runs seasonally, as a short cut, the route south of the Skye bridge. The white-bearded operator clocked me as a Lewisman by the way I placed my foot on the rail. "Aye, you're right," I said. "And it must be interesting water here, when the wind drives all that sea in to meet the tide."

"Yes," he said, "It's open all right. In fact, on a very clear day you can almost see the glint?"

"Barra Head?" I asked.

"No," he said. "The sun glancing off the helmet of the Statue of Liberty."

Crofters on Skye, c.1890

Skye: touring the Misty Isle

*A rainbow arc of bridge delivers you straight to the 1970s 'Skye
Crofters' Motorway'. To glimpse this unparalleled island in a day,
hurtle round the loop taken by coach tours. A short run, through
gorse and spruce, brings you to Broadford Bay, with fine views of
islands to the north, up the Inner Sound. Travel on. The coast road
skirts Loch Ainort, where on a rough day the wind whips water into
little twisters. Then climb into the bleak pass through the rounded
form of the Red Cuillins. The fearsome crags of the Black Cuillins are
away to the west, but these lower hills, too, are impressive.*

*At Sligachan, the old tryst of cattle drovers, bear right to
Portree, a neat town, its harbour guarded by cliffs. There's no time
to take the northern loop unless you have longer, so the remarkable
pinnacle of the Storr Rock and the strange tipped-up form of
the Quirang will go unseen to day-trippers, along with the deep
horseshoe cove of Uig. Instead a crofting landscape of cropped
moor and ordered, strip-like fields unfolds between Bernisdale and
Edinbane, with a scatter of low, traditional houses.*

*Down to Dunvegan: your driver will take you to the grey tower
of the castle, its gardens, the seal rocks, the precious Fairy Flag.
The magical coral beaches lie beyond. Too soon you will be heading
south, catching enrapturing glimpses of sea lochs, islands, skerries
to the west, hurtling past prehistoric brochs and souterrains,
threading round tight bends below cliffs, where burns cascade
white water after rain. The whole Cuillin Ridge will be laid out
before you in the distance: fine viewed from the north but never as
wonderful as seen, snow-capped, from the south, in morning light
from Ord, or Dunscaith Castle at Tokavaig, or from remote, end-
of-the-world Elgol. You'd need more time to wander to the Fairy
Pools, or drive down Glen Brittle, or climb to that enticing ridge.*

*Some days you may see only the intriguing outlines of these
spectacular features through battalions of raindrops, squadrons of
snow showers or the ever-encircling mist. But Skye is unforgettable,
whenever you experience it.*   Fi Martynoga

THE OUTER LANDS

Outer Hebrides, Orkney, Shetland

As a man who was born and brought up in Stornoway, Isle of Lewis, I suggest that each of these more populated outer archipelagos maintains a distinct identity. The range of cultural elements is at least as wide as the range of landscapes. We move from the Roman Catholic Southern Isles of the Outer Hebrides, through Presbyterian Harris and Lewis to the more recent Norse colonies of Orkney and Shetland. There are different accents of Gaelic from the Uists to Lewis and there is a town patois clinging on in Stornoway. The Doric influence is evident in Orcadian dialect and the Norse still strong in the Shetland tongue.

As I write this in January 2015, in a week when winds peaked at 113mph over Lewis, we look ahead to a week where disruptions to ferries and flights can be expected. That's the difference between living on a landmass connected by causeway or bridge and living on one which is not. Cranes swing over Stornoway harbour, struggling to install the infrastructure for a new and larger ferry. They are trying to make up for the time lost to a series of storms. People will remember the names of past ferries on all the islands and the routine crossings which became epics. The 'new boat', which will take over the North Minch route to Ullapool in 2015, will carry the same name as the boat which joined Stornoway to the railheads of Kyle and Mallaig just after the Second World War – Loch Seaforth.

Each of these three groups of outer islands is like a country in itself. The Western Isles shelters around 27,000 people, though the population is still falling. Orkney has a more stable population of around 20,000 and Shetland too holds on at about 22,000. Each has its own body of music, of visual art and literature. Each topic on each group of islands warrants more than one book to itself. Coasts and the surrounding sea are strong elements in all. The storytelling heritage is huge. Prehistoric marks, from chambered cairns to standing stones to brochs, are found on the shorelines of outlying islands as well as the main landmasses with their bustling harbours. But the harbour towns of Stornoway, Stromness and Lerwick have innovative arts centres on their skylines as well as industrial architecture.

The scale of these three island groups is too vast to summarise. Instead I would like to present a small, biased, sample.

Outer Hebrides

Mingulay lies to the south of Barra. The landing place is a steep sandy beach on the east side. The snug forms of stone houses with turf roofs are so settled in the landscape that you have to look and blink and look again to see them. MacPhee's Hill is steep behind them and the west side falls away to fearsome cliffs. But these were the secrets to settlement in this exposed

The central stones at Callanish, Isle of Lewis

place. There was not sufficient ground to feed the village but the cliffs provided seabirds, as did the rock stacks of St Kilda and Fair Isle and Foula. People live on in these Shetland Isles but not in Mingulay, nor the Monachs, nor Hirta, nor Scarp, nor Mealasta, nor Pabbay Mor, nor Little Bernera nor North Rona, all out from the Hebrides.

Oral culture, especially song, is much stronger in this group than instrumental music, though piping is still strong in the Uists and the cheery melodeon bands have had a revival in North Lewis. All the settlements down the length of the Western Isles are on the shoreline except for the unique inland village (now Achmore and Lochganvich), said to have been a place of exile. This exception was used to trip up a Tory candidate ('from away') at a recent general election. The question from the floor was, "And would the candidate care to comment on the proposals to expand the pier at Achmore?" She declared herself fully in support of this initiative, or so the new legend goes.

There are long stretches of white sands on the west shore of most of the islands in the Outer Hebrides. Aircraft still land on the cockle strand on Barra. Luskentyre on Harris looks over to Taransay, one of the many islands which maintained a population until well into the 20th century. The Viking-created Lewis Chessmen, probably carved in Trondheim from walrus ivory, were found in a cache in the dunes of Uig sands further north on Lewis.

It is the contrasts of landscape which make the Outer Hebrides unique. The terrain seems to alter with the speed of the changing skies which sweep over it. This is often caught in songs and

stories but was missed or evaded by the would-be developers of what would have been the largest superquarry in Europe, located in Lingerbay, Harris. A 'landscape consultant' quoted from a scattering of literary sources, including Sir Walter Scott, to rubbish

Remembering the *Iolaire*

A few months after the end of the First World War, Stornoway, the capital of Harris and Lewis and the largest town in the Hebrides, was the scene of a most poignant tragedy. Late on

New Year's Eve, the Iolaire, an Admiralty yacht acting as a troop carrier to bring sailors home from the war, left Kyle of Lochalsh in deteriorating weather. In the early hours of 1919 and just at the entrance to Stornoway's harbour, she hit the notorious rocks known locally as 'The Beasts of Holm'. She quickly sank.

Although within sight of the lights of the town and just yards from the shore, only 82 of the 283 men recorded as being on board managed to reach the shore. Of these, 40 were saved by an extraordinary feat of strength and bravery when a Lewis man, John F Macleod from Ness, swam ashore with a hauling line from the rigging. Using this, some of the sailors were able to heave themselves through the waves. Another forty-two gained safety by their own efforts. Most, though, were weighed down by their heavy uniforms and boots, and few of them could swim.

The agony of the men, snatched by vicious seas so near to home, and of their families who found their bodies washed up later that morning, still resonates. The memorial to the dead at Holm, just above the town, is a place of reverence and pilgrimage. A further reminder is a pillar marking the site of the wreck, which can be seen on the approach to Stornoway Harbour.

Many Gaelic songs and poems were written to commemorate this unthinkable loss of so many of the young men of the islands. For the centenary of the wreck of the Iolaire, at the start of 2019, the Scottish group Skipinnish composed a new song which glimpses something of the agony of the men who thought they were safe 'Sailing west and worlds away / from the futile fields of war'.   Fi Martynoga the aesthetic qualities of the bare east side of Harris. Scott saw it through drizzle on a brief visit, so the mountain tops would have been cut off short. Some days he might have quite liked the romance of that but his comments suggest that he was having a classical day, longing for a more subdued Nature.

If you walk 'the funeral path', which takes you from the bare bays of east Harris to the lush machair of Luskentyre on the west, you are aware that the grey east and turquoise west complement each other. In case you wonder at the significance of the cairns along the way, these were dram stops for those who carried a coffin to a place where there was sufficient soil to cover it. There's quite a lot of them.

None of the hills in either south or north Harris is quite over the 3,000-foot figure, but most of them rise sharply from sea level. Their shoulders provide fine ridge walks but, like the high ground of Skye, these are now well documented. If I were to choose just one coastal walk, it would be the cliff path that snakes through the tumbled gneiss north of Hushinish at the end of the twistiest road you are ever likely to drive. You look across to high Scarp, an island now dotted with a few houses occupied only in the summer. Its lost ceilidh culture is evoked in Angus Duncan's excellent memoir, *Hebridean Island, Memories of Scarp.*

I used to cross over to stay in the holiday house of a German composer, Diethelm Zuckmantel, who was setting some of my poems to music at the time. This allowed me to experience the walk across to the otter-tracked beach of Kearstay – although I later found these lines from my notes taken on one visit to Scarp:

> *I don't dare walk this sand.*
> *Tide re-makes the Sound*
> *twice most days.*

There is an organisation called The Islands Book Trust which arranges boat trips to the less accessible islands, like Scarp and the Monachs, and promotes discussion and publication of the literature linked to them. Back across the Sound of Scarp on Harris, you come off the rocky track to pass a keeper's cottage and notice padded turfs by a freshwater loch. Then you meet the bay of Loch

Cravadale. With luck, you might see the thick speckled backs and stainless glint of sea trout, powering from cross-currents to glide over stones. They are driving in to a loch set in a steep-sided glen. You are likely to see both species of eagles and see or hear deer. One recent sighting noted a conference of seven sea eagles on the boulders of Cravadale.

If you are fortunate you will be able to camp there or continue to Loch Resort where you can try roasting mussels on a driftwood fire. This was one of the many settlements more accessible by boat than road. Perhaps you will be able to continue on, round Loch Tamnavay and looking out to Mealasta Island, until you meet the end of another road. I walked out from the road-end at Islavig, past Brenish, only a few weeks ago:

> *how yellow, gold and even white are*
> *all necessary but not sufficient*
> *to indicate the sweating beach*
> *on Mealasta island*
>
> *how green, even male mallard green*
> *even shag green under the crest*
> *are not strong enough to say the colour*
> *of the suck of the seep in that geo*
>
> *some of the illuminations*
> *came on for us*
> *even though the days are longer*
> *   now*
> *– Mealasval sulked but*
> *   Suinaval shone*

Buses do run and you might be surprised at how many of the island's road-ends can be reached by public transport.

Stone circle at Stenness, Orkney

Orkney

Orkney was the Vikings' breadbasket. There are still major farms and the green often runs all the way to the cliffs. The marks of prehistoric farmers are dense on all the complex coastlines. Orkney Mainland boasts a major harbour on both the west side at Stromness and the east side at Kirkwall, the gateway to the North Sea. Again, the range within the geography is huge, from the cliffs that fall away at Yesnaby on the south-west of Mainland to the beaches of Sanday, which looks as if it could disappear given a few inches' rise in sea level.

The Island of Hoy is not typical. Its landscape is more like the Highlands. Hoy rises as if in a Japanese print, out across the white rips of tide, from Stromness. You look from St John's Head to the Old Man, separated by years of assaulting spray. Similar forces have shaped the huge rounded boulders of Rackwick, each one like a work of Barbara Hepworth carried over from The Pier Arts Centre across the Sound. There is a counter tone of smaller rolling pebbles.

Yet, within a few cables of Hoy, lying between the high ground and the approaches to Stromness, lies the low farmland of Graemsay (not to be confused with other islands of very similar names off Benbecula and out from Akureyri, Iceland, above the

Arctic circle.) I crossed by ferry during the Orkney Storytelling Festival with Bryce Wilson, illustrator of Tom Muir's excellent gathering of Orcadian stories, *The Mermaid Bride*. Bryce pointed me to a low-lying modest stone building with an intact roof of turf, set daringly close to the lapping tide. I thought it was a boathouse. It had been home to his own grandparents. We walked the rough coastal path to the lighthouse. Here the water changes as fast as the skies. I've navigated in and out of Hoy Sound several times in different craft and it has never been the same experience twice. This day, I was mesmerised by the drawing eddies, close inshore. I'd been well warned not to even attempt stemming the tide here by trying to enter the Sound from the west if I missed the last of the east-going stream. You might be lucky and get spat back out but you might get caught in the ever-shifting forces close to predatory black reefs. You can see why this area is at the forefront of research into tidal and wave energy… and why it is not going to be easy to harness these forces.

Almost every resident of the island turned out for our gathering in the hall. There are teleworkers as well as those who work with tactile materials. If the cakes and the banter are anything to go by, folk are making a real effort at maintaining a community here.

That was only a couple of months back from this date of January 2015. Now, I'm looking back much further, to notes of walks round the northern part of Orkney, back in the 1980s. I don't think the territory has changed much.

Sanday

Expansive skies
as in Dutch masters
but these are faster –
shifting light tones.

Sea colours assault
both shores and eyes.
A lot of angry white
breaking from brilliance.

Dry dykes could never
hold that water out
so grazings and furrows
are backspaced
a field-fathom

but lichened slabs,
cemented just high enough
to make muted roofs,
stay-put
on built frames.

Gales ruffle skins
of sand and walls;
of cattle and dwellings
and pass over all.

Shetland

More than any of the other archipelagos, Shetland can be seen as its own country. Like Orkney, its literature has a vast range in time from Norse saga to contemporary poetry. The annual Wordplay festival, in the modernist Mareel performance space, places the voices of these islands in an international context. Its music has moved from a firm traditional basis, with a strong legacy of fiddle tunes, to daring crossovers with the contemporary.

Even its fleets of sailing craft have been developed from a shared Norse ancestry to include elements of modern technology. They sail their 'Shetland models' to the limit in regattas, and their rowing fleet competed with those of Faroe long before the idea of coastal rowing was taken up on other Scottish coasts.

As a walker or angler or sailor, the choice of routes round deep-cut 'voes' (inlets) is vast. The infrastructure of transport, schools and libraries is impressive, showing prudent investment of oil-related revenues. Lerwick harbour is a vital commercial port as well as a haven for commercial and leisure craft.

Faced with this range of contrasts, I can only share the briefest of samples. The total mileage of Shetland's coastlines is estimated at close to 1,700. Here are two remembered landfalls, both on the eastern side of the group:

Mousa

There are scheduled boat trips to include a walk ashore on Mousa, which lies between Sumburgh Head (at the southern tip of Shetland Mainland) and Lerwick harbour (about midway up the east side). I was able to step ashore as crew for my friend Edward Anker. Ed fitted out the bare hull of a 28ft coastal cruising boat and sailed it from New Zealand to St Kilda via the Patagonian channels. He was glad of company for a detour to Shetland before continuing on his planned circumnavigation. We had put in to Westray, towards the north of Orkney. Instead of being sensible and staying there to take part in the local skiff racing, we attempted to reach Fair Isle harbour before a forecast northerly gale hit. We did make the entrance but Ed judged it unsafe in the developing gale and we beat on through the night towards Sumburgh.

We lay to heavy anchor tackle in the bight close to the airport to recover before sneaking in at high water to a small boat haven. We had a couple of nights there waiting for a wind shift and were made most welcome. A fisherman passed us a bag with four live brown crab as we departed, hoping to call in at Mousa. After our hammering, pushing the boat hard on the wind to get this far north, we had an easy sail into the lee of the island. Ed went ashore first to explore the Mousa Broch, one of the most intact to be found anywhere. He ate both meat and fish but was squeamish when it came to bones and shells. I did the deed with the crabs as I kept anchor watch and set the vessel's hammer and knife to work. Three were dispatched, boiled and dressed by the time the skipper returned. I asked him to look the other way now but he said no, the last one, still lively, could do her bit to maintain the population. We had new potatoes and salad and I could not imagine eating any better. Then I stepped to the dinghy to take my turn.

You come ashore to a rug of sea pink on each rounded rock. The track is firm. Then you are humbled, looking at the balancing of small and larger stones which has lasted for centuries. They are like the ancient verses which describe voyages on routes where there is no prior knowledge of the islands you might sight next.

Baltasound

We took the buoyed channel into the lagoon at Out Skerries before taking a different exit route out towards Unst. Out Skerries is often an anchorage for those on transit to or from Norway. But we were first bound further towards the top of Shetland. Before you make landfall at Baltasound, you note the heavy timber remains of a system of piers erected to host the black sailing ships which set miles of drift-nets to supply the international trade in herring. The history of more modest craft, which fished to feed the mouths of local people, is set out in the exemplary boat museum at the next bay to the north.

You can hike or drive or cycle from that to the eerie site of a huge listening installation, another piece of architectural archaeology now, marking the peak of the Cold War. But Ed and I were driven there by a kind fellow sailor, a native of Hoy, who had settled up this way. We strolled over the hill, dodging the diving bonxies. From here, we could look out to yet another white-painted lighthouse, still in commission. Muckle Flugga Lighthouse, designed by David and Thomas Stevenson, was made permanent in 1858 and was manned till 1995. Our friend had seen the forecasts. We were unlikely to be sailing round the most northerly island in the UK, this trip. This was as close as we could get, with the wind rising again.

You can also see the shore station for Muckle Flugga, set up a voe on Unst. This terrain is said to have shaped the map of the treasure island dreamed up by Robert Louis Stevenson, who had visited the site with his uncle and father when they built the lighthouse. So that imagined land is informed by the actual observation of one of the countless islands lying out from the Scottish

Rough seas off Unst: firing the imagination of many a writer

mainland. For me the split narrative technique of *Treasure Island* is a master stroke. It foreshadows use of similar techniques in later literature and was much admired by great thinkers and storytellers, such as the Argentine Jorge Luis Borges, at a time where it seemed fashionable to dismiss the 'romances' of RLS in the universities of Scotland. Strangely enough I'd been introduced to the work of Borges by the Orcadian, George Mackay Brown, a rooted island man widely travelled in mental outlook.

I could not help thinking back to Erraid and Stevenson's *Kidnapped*, a great romance for children of any age. Sometimes the Scottish psyche seems to be a perpetual skirmish between the prudent David Balfour and the headstrong Alan Breck.

Ian Stephen

St Kilda

Lying 40 miles west of the Outer Hebrides, for decades St Kilda has been the ultimate destination for explorers of the remotest corners of Britain. The lonely archipelago captured people's imaginations in 1930 when newspapers reported the evacuation of the existing population from what had become a desperate struggle for existence. For many years after being abandoned, St Kilda was visited only by the privileged or adventurous few, but now increasing numbers of explorers are finding their way there.

Although landings are never guaranteed, just the sight of St Kilda from the sea can be an awe-inspiring experience. The island landscape is characterised by a jagged skyline above stupendous cliffs, with spectacular sea stacks offshore and clouds of birds overhead in the nesting season. The only safe landing place is in Village Bay on Hirta, the main island. Here visitors are surprised to find that first they have to walk past the staff accommodation buildings at a modern radar tracking station.

This aside, the layout of the island is very much as it was a century ago. The village plan was reorganised in the 19th century, and long crofts stretch up the hillside to the village street, where six of the houses have been re-roofed for seasonal use. Everywhere hundreds of small stone-built storehouses, known as cleits, dot the landscape (including the one that once housed the exiled Lady Grange), and Soay sheep, a breed surviving from centuries ago, graze the slopes. There are no trees, but there is much else to delight naturalists – puffins, huge gannet colonies, fulmars and the St Kilda wren, a unique sub-species. On the north side of the island, ruined structures and field walls provide glimpses of even earlier landscapes, and everywhere, given clear conditions, the views are breathtaking. Appropriately, St Kilda is owned by the National Trust for Scotland, and the quality of both its natural and historical features have recently justified it being recognised by UNESCO as a dual World Heritage Site.

Chris and Margaret Knowles

ISLAND JAUNTS

There are plenty of smaller islands on both the east and west coast that are easy to get to for the day from a variety of different starting points. Below are some of our favourites.

Inchcolm

If you tire of Edinburgh in the summer, it is possible to transport yourself to another world within two hours. It's a small one but so full of interest you will not spend much time looking back over the water at the city.

Lying in the Firth of Forth, this island is almost as delightful as Iona but much less well known or visited. Its abbey, founded in the 12th century on a site already used by Culdee hermits, was dedicated to Saint Columba. Like Iona, it has been the burial place of kings and other nobles, and of large numbers of Danish soldiers. A 'hogback' stone, now preserved in the visitors' centre, is probably a memorial to one of their leaders. It was Sweyn Forkbeard, King of the Danes, who paid handsomely for the privilege of committing their bones to an island grave, where neither dogs nor wolves might exhume them.

What is remarkable about the abbey is the survival of many of its buildings, intact, and even with roofs. The octagonal chapter house, the cloisters with refectory and dormitory above them, and part of the church can all be seen, almost as if the Reformation never happened. Being offshore, they avoided the excesses of reforming mobs, and the place remained partly used as a residence, the rest of it being allowed to slide into ruin. Its charm is in this state of decay, which allows the historical imagination full play, and also in its situation. The greensward and scatter of trees of this tiny island are compelling: so near to Edinburgh, yet worlds apart.

You get to Inchcolm on a boat from South Queensferry, cruising along the Forth. It takes less than an hour and gives you an hour and a half to explore. There are First and Second World War fortifications, the former Navy, Army and Air Force Institutes (NAAFI) building being the gift shop run by Historic Scotland, which has the custody of the buildings. Fulmars, gulls and terns breed successfully on the island, as it lacks terrestrial predators like stoats and hedgehogs.

The Isle of May

The watercolours of Keith Brockie, particularly one of an eider duck on her nest, introduced me and many others to the extraordinary wildlife of this place. He was artist in residence on the island in the early 1980s and his watercolours record the riches of the summer populations of breeding seabirds, the carpets of sea pink and sea campion, and the ever-present grey seals on the rocks. It was a further 30 years before I got myself there. I regretted not having made the effort, as it has enough charm and interest to make it worthy of many visits.

A boat from Anstruther takes 45 minutes to deliver you to the Isle of May jetty. You are making a journey taken by pilgrims over many centuries. In medieval times the chapel was dedicated to St Adrian, though it was probably founded as early as the 9th century. It was built into a prehistoric burial mound, so Dark Age bones still mingle there with Neolithic ashes. Later, lighthouse keepers and their families crossed the water to the island regularly. In 1636 a beacon was established to mark May's reefs, so dangerous to shipping. It was the first lighthouse in Scotland, yet the coal-fired beacon itself brought disaster to one family of keepers in 1791, when fumes from smouldering clinker outside their window poisoned them. There is a romantic twist to this sorry tale, as the only survivor, a child of three, grew up to marry the boy who rescued her.

Another first for the island (and for Scotland) was the foundation of a bird observatory in 1934, using the building that was formerly a second lighthouse. The observatory was set up for the study of migrants which use the island as a brief pit-stop. It still functions today, manned by volunteers, who net and ring hundreds of birds each year. Volunteers also help the wardens provided by Scottish Natural Heritage, who manage the site as a National Nature Reserve, to protect the other wildlife. Puffins breed well on May, because rabbits introduced by monks in the 14th century keep the grass short, and even provide some of the burrows the birds need for nesting. Razorbills, shag, fulmars, kittiwakes and gulls also nest here, and terns in some seasons, depending on the supply of sand eels and other small fish in the Forth.

It's easy to walk round the whole island, which is only 45 hectares, in the time given you by the boatman. You should take the opportunity to explore every corner. I recall peeping over a low cliff at the tarbet, or isthmus, between the main island and Rona, which is almost a separate isle, to find a seal peering back at me, only yards away. About 400 live there all year, but the numbers swell to nearly 4,000 in the autumn breeding season. The pictures show the whole place a-ripple with seals. You can't visit then, as the island is only open from May to October, but you can watch on screens in the Seabird Centre in North Berwick. These are connected to webcams on May that record much of the annual activity of the wildlife there.

Volunteers can stay in parts of the lighthouse, built in 1816 by the Stevenson family with castellations suggesting a Gothic castle. Its tower still functions as the lighthouse, though it has been computer-controlled since the last keeper left in 1989.

Opposite: a sketch of the original lighthouse on the Isle of May

The distinctive shape of Ailsa Craig

Ailsa Craig

The small open boats that ply over the 10 miles of choppy sea between Girvan and the great rock of Ailsa Craig are not for the faint-hearted. Theoretically, they work year-round, but in practice the weather dictates whether it is possible to sail. I made the journey on a sunny September day after a gale. A big sea was running and the boatman was in two minds about whether to take us. But he did, and we smashed against the waves for what seemed like a very long time, the great granite plug of 'Paddy's Milestone' seeming to dance ahead of us and only very slowly to grow larger. As we drew near to the lighthouse jetty it was still rough, so we circled the great rock, admiring its high cliffs of hard granite, traditionally used to make curling stones. One quarry is still in use, with harvests of the favoured 'blue hone' stone made every few years, when the local factory runs out of material.

The cliffs are guano-streaked from the seabird nurseries. Ailsa is Britain's third-largest breeding colony of gannets and is now owned and managed by the RSPB. By September when I visited the birds had already started their migration south, but there were still large numbers of them plummeting into the sea around the boat as we completed the 4.5-mile circumnavigation and drew up to the jetty. We lurched ashore and scampered up to the lighthouse, with its solid walled enclosure, another Stevenson achievement. The light was fired by gas from a works still visible. Coal was winched up to it in trucks along an early railway. Another set of tracks brought the blue hone granite down to the jetty.

We wanted to see Ailsa Castle, a 16th-century tower built by the Hamilton family at the time of anxiety about Spanish invasion. Its solid vaults were later used as a prison and it still stands nearly three storeys high. After that, we scrambled up to the highest point of the island, enjoying the grassland, with sheepsbit and tormentil still flowering. The wind was wild and we kept back from the edge, having read of the Victorian lady who was swept over the cliff by a gust but survived the fearful fall when her skirts acted as a parachute!

Time for exploration was soon up and we descended to the boat past feral billy goats on a crag. The old tea-room that was famous for its scones is no longer there, though whether the animals are descendants of the tea-room's milk herd of nannies is not clear.

The wind seemed to drop, so we had expectations of an easier passage home. But the wild west coast wasn't going to let us off lightly. Although the wind was with us, the tide was against us, making for a choppy sea, so we butted back against the waves and were pleased to make landfall before the sun set on an exhilarating day.

Raasay

Raasay, off the east coast of Skye and accessible by car ferry from Sconser, is an island with a distinctive skyline. Its flat-topped hill, Dun Caan, is like a miniature of one of MacLeod's Tables on Skye. Early travellers walked round the island in a day, but as it is 14 miles long and three wide, they can't have had much time to enjoy the place. Raasay House was formerly a gentleman's residence visited by James Boswell and Samuel Johnson in 1773. The latter found "nothing but civility, elegance and plenty". In the last 40 years it has seen dereliction, revival, community buy-out, and fire, but it's now been totally refurbished as holiday accommodation with an outdoor centre, a café, bar and restaurant. Tourism is the primary earner in this place that used to rely on its mineral wealth, fishing in the deep waters that surround it, and crofting.

On a day trip you can taste some of the island's pleasures. Raasay House is just north of the principal village, Inverarish, where the ferry docks. Several special things linger in my memory from my first visit. On its battery you can see the old cannon and the stone mermaids from the island's heyday. Nearby is a fine Pictish stone which shows a Christian cross that may connect it to Saint Moluag in the 6th century. Below the cross are some more enigmatic symbols, a crescent and a broken sword, as seen on Pictish stones elsewhere in Scotland.

Next I recall travelling north on the rambling one-track road to Brochel Castle, a marvellously picturesque ruin standing on a pinnacle above the sea. Beyond that is the famous two-mile stretch of road built by hand by Calum MacLeod between 1964–74. He and his wife were the last residents of Arnish, the most northerly settlement on the island. They had despaired of the local council ever providing them with a road, so Calum took on the work singlehandedly, using only a pick, shovel and wheelbarrow.

If you take pleasure in wildlife, the flowers of Raasay are rewarding, with a variety of orchids in season, saxifrages, mountain avens and other alpines. Sea eagles, otters and smaller beasts, like the unique Raasay vole, can also be found. Another simple pleasure, if you can find a way down the eastern cliffs (at Fearns, for example) is the mottled beach pebbles on the shore. I remember, too, a fisherman's hut made from an upturned boat, but can find no mention of it in contemporary accounts, so maybe it has decayed away. Finally, you should not leave the island without honouring its poet, Sorley MacLean, who was born at Ostaig, although he spent most of his life on the mainland of Skye.

Bute

The Isle of Bute is a curious hybrid sort of place. This stems from its geology: the Highland Boundary Fault runs across it, making the northern part rough and hilly, whilst the southern half is lower-lying agricultural land. Yet it is the human marks, or lack of them, that really create the split personality.

Rothesay, the principal port and town where you dock on the ferry from Wemyss Bay, south of Greenock, is an extraordinary creation. As the boat came in I admired Victorian houses of all shapes and extravagances lined up around the bay. Some are plain-fronted villas painted in seaside colours. Others, taller, with fancy balconies and palm trees in their gardens, speak of the heyday of the town as a holiday resort for the people of Glasgow. It was very fashionable in its time, with smart shops, a winter garden

(the pagoda is now a discovery centre), and
magnificent public lavatories, which are
still functioning in all their Victorian
splendour and are something of an
attraction in themselves. In the cen-
tre of the town is the fine ruin of a 13th-century castle. If you
climb to its wall walks, you will have fine views of the town and the
bay, with the hills of the mainland beyond.

Like Rothesay, the chief man-made attraction on the island is
also Victorian. Mount Stewart is probably the best and most lav-
ish example of a neo-Gothic great house in the whole of Scotland.
It was built in the late 1870s, after an earlier house belonging to
the Marquis of Bute was destroyed by fire. The architect, Rowand
Anderson (1834–1921), also designed the National Portrait
Gallery in Edinburgh and the two buildings have some similari-
ties. Both of them are of red sandstone, and make reference to an
early Gothic style, with a hint of the Doge's Palace about them. If
you are a fan of the Edinburgh building, you must visit this island
landmark. All of it is lavishly appointed and decorated, the marble
hall and chapel exceptionally so. The gardens are kept up in the
traditional manner, with a team of gardeners looking after the
kitchen garden, rock garden, walks, pinetum, chickens and apiary.

You can travel directly to the southern tip of the island to
see the ruins of the medieval St Blane's church and then circle
north on the west side where you can find the best sandy beaches.
Ettrick Bay was another Victorian resort and maintained its pop-
ularity until the 1930s, when the little railway that connected it
to Rothesay closed down. The beach lies at the southern end of
the wildest, most Highland part of the island, where you really
do get a feel of the Hebrides and experience the other nature
of the Isle of Bute. However, to do so you will have to walk, for
the little road soon peters out. Only the A886 on the east gets to
the northern end of the island, where a small ferry connects to
Colintraive, on a finger of the southernmost peninsula of Argyll.
It's a good stepping-off place for the Highlands that avoids Loch
Lomondside, but you do have to pay to get on and off Bute by
ferry. The Kyles of Bute are so narrow that you scarcely notice the
passage, except in the purse!

Arran

Arran for me is an engraving from the *Universal British Traveller* of 1779, showing, "Loch Ranza: the Manner of Taking the Basking Shark." It's on my bathroom wall where I look at it daily, admiring the two sailing ships but grieving for the shark, which is being harpooned from a rowing boat. They must have been such a tempting resource, so large, yet lazy enough in their movements to be easy to kill. Fortunately they were not quite fished to extinction and can still be seen off Arran in the summer (see Fauna, page 37).

Of course, I have been there and seen Lochranza for myself, with its tall castle ruin on a spit of sand and shingle – the castle that provided the inspiration for the Tintin comic *The Black Island.* The road from the ferry dock at Brodick leads north through the waterfront villages of Corrie and Sannox, where otter may sometimes be seen nearby either settlement. The landscape beyond these is overburdened with sitka spruce plantation, but you eventually get out on to the hills and are quickly rewarded with jagged rocks and soaring mountain peaks enough to gratify those 18th-century travellers (Universal or not) with the thrill of The Sublime.

The geological wealth of the island is considerable (see Geology, page 12), and school parties are often to be seen spotting glacial features, Hutton's Unconformity, the different types and ages of rock. You descend through more pleasing woods to the natural harbour of Lochranza, a square inlet that on a calm day looks more like a lake than a sea loch. Its attractive village was founded on herring fishing, later on tourism and, most recently, whisky: a distillery was founded here in the 1990s. The pier has recently been reinstated and is now a summer calling point for the paddle steamer *Waverley* from Glasgow, as well as the smaller ferry from Kintyre. I saw red deer on shore of the loch where they feed on seaweed. I'm told they can sometimes be seen standing up to their knees in water. They're certainly often found on the small golf course, which doubles up as a campsite, and otters, seals and golden eagles are all frequently spotted from here, too.

If you continue around the point from Lochranza to the west coast road, you'll find Catacol, a hamlet best known for the waterfront row of white houses called the Twelve Apostles. They were built

Lochranza and the 1770s basking shark (see opposite)

in the mid-19th century to house crofters evicted from elsewhere on the island during the Clearances. From there, the road hugs the pebbly shore and gives you fine views of the Mull of Kintyre.

When you reach Auchagallon, where there is a prehistoric stone circle, turn left and the wee hill road called The String will take you back to Brodick. Or you can potter on round the whole edge of the island, to encounter Blackwaterfoot with its pretty bridge and bit of harbour, and finally Lamlash, the island's largest village. In the bay overlooked by the village lies Holy Island, now a Buddhist retreat. It's possible to go across for the day, but you are asked not to take dogs or alcohol with you, and not to kindle fire.

When you finally circle back to Brodick you will have the castle and its grounds to look forward to. Although it was founded as early as the 12th century and extended over the next four hundred years, very little of the early structure survives. The place was substantially rebuilt for the Duke of Hamilton, to plans drawn up by James Gillespie Graham around 1840, so you don't get the medieval castle experience so much as that of the 19th-century great house. The National Trust for Scotland, which took over Brodick Castle in 1957, presents the property very well, with its full complement of opulent rooms, as well as all the kitchens and domestic offices. The gardens, too, are very fine as they benefit from the mild temperatures Arran enjoys because of the Gulf Stream.

For the botanist, Arran has good plants to seek out, including the three sub-species of Sorbus, the Arran, the cut-leaved, and the Catacol whitebeams (*S. arranensis, S. pseudofennica amd S. pseudomeinichii*), which are rare but protected in Glen Diomhan. Many other more common plants flower in profusion during summer above the beaches and on the cliffs of the island (see Plants, page 50).

Fi Martynoga

SEVEN

GREAT
DAYS OUT

EYEMOUTH

Location and transport

In the south-east of Scotland, an hour's drive on the A1 from Edinburgh but served by a regular bus service, Perryman's 253.

Essence of the place

A working fishing town with a sense of bustle about its harbour slipways, boat repair shops and ice plant, it has a sheltered beach, good museums, and excellent walks, especially along cliff paths above magnificent rocks.

What to see

You can enjoy the harbour with its resident seals, the beach, rock pools and short cliff walks from the town. The main street offers art galleries and the harbour a ship's chandlers. There are plenty of cafés and pubs to choose from. The Eyemouth Museum, in an old church near the centre, has good displays of the town's long history of fishing, and a tapestry commemorating the 1881 disaster when a sudden storm caught the fishing fleet at sea: 129 Eyemouth fishermen were drowned. Their widows and children are further commemorated by a bronze sculpture that will ultimately depict each one of them. A sculpture trail along the coast offers children an opportunity to do small brass-rubbings that build up a picture of the fishing fleet in harbour. Eyemouth Maritime Centre houses an interesting display of boats from around the world. Gunsgreen House is a fine building which tells the story of smuggling in the town.

What to do

Longer walks along the rolling cliff tops above remarkable rock formations are not to be missed, either south through the golf course to Burnmouth, or north-west towards St Abbs, both of them attractive villages with harbours. Get the bus back into town. To visit Siccar Point (page 11) start at Cove (served by the 253 bus) from where it is a 10km round walk. St Abbs itself is a nature reserve, and the sea off the promontory a marine reserve much enjoyed by divers. A boat operates from the harbour there to take both sightseers and divers to the best spots.

NORTH BERWICK

Location and transport

On the south shore of the Firth of Forth, on the A198, 20 miles north-east of Edinburgh with a reasonably frequent train service. Travelling by bike or car, you could visit one of the many beautiful sandy beaches of East Lothian.

Essence of the place

A pretty Victorian seaside resort with a much older core, a harbour and the relatively new Seabird Centre.

What to see

The town is simply laid out, its High Street one back from the sea. There are interesting shops and cafés to explore after a bracing walk along the two fine beaches and a visit to the harbour, home of the East Lothian Yacht Club. The harbour is 19th century but on a medieval site. Two ruined churches and several fine houses from the 18th and early 19th centuries give the town some architectural distinction. The Scottish Seabird Centre houses good displays and a network of cameras trained on seabird nesting sites on the Bass Rock, the Isle of May, and other islands in the Forth. It's well worth a visit.

What to do

Climb North Berwick Law, the volcanic plug behind the town, to get a superb bird's-eye view of the whole place, and a great sense of the Firth of Forth and Fife beyond. The whalebone arch (now fibreglass!) commemorates the town's history as a whaling port. The Museum of Flight is a few miles inland and the magnificent Tantallon Castle only a couple of miles east along the coast. Go further to Tyningham to find coastal woods and some dunes, or west to Aberlady for excellent opportunities to see estuarine birds

and wild flowers. Beaches like Yellowcraigs and Gullane have good dune flora and sea buckthorn is common along the coast.

PORTOBELLO

Location and transport

A short way out of town to the east, on the shores of the Firth of Forth, Portobello is easily accessible by bus (26, 42, 45 & 124), and now by train, from central Edinburgh.

Essence of the place

The settlement, grown from the name given to a cottage by a sailor returning from the battle of Porto Bello in Panama, during the War of Jenkins Ear, is a faded Victorian watering place and former summer holiday destination for Central Belters. Its pier is long gone, but it still offers more than a mile of esplanade and wide sands, which can be a refreshing walk after city streets. In recent years Porty has been experiencing a boom as Edinburgh residents seek out the extra space, sea air and the more relaxed, arty, community-minded vibe that now feels like quite a contrast from the festivals and AirBnB tourism-led city centre.

What to see

The High Street parallels the coast, and you approach the beach down any one of a number of small cul-de-sac streets, which run at right angles from it. The best of them have fine early 19th-century houses, long popular with Edinburgh's alternative middle classes. There are enough of these younger people to support artisan bakers, bistros and some interesting cafés, all of them within easy reach of the beach, and a welcome recent addition is an independent bookshop, on the High Street. Do not miss the beautifully restored Bath House at the sea end of Bath Street. If you want simpler pleasures, there are still fish and chip shops and an amusement arcade.

What to do

Treat yourself to a swim and then a luxurious Turkish Bath in the Bath House. Visit RowPorty to try your hand at rowing in an Iain Oughtred St Ayles skiff (see page 211, Coastal Rowing). Go a mile inland to the

National Trust for Scotland's Newhailes, a 17th-century house that has been preserved much as its early 20th-century owners left it, or walk the couple of miles along the coast to Musselburgh to visit the newly refurbished museum and buy ice cream from one of the most famous Italian makers in Scotland.

EAST NEUK

location and transport

On the north shore of the Firth of Forth, east of Glenrothes. A car is easiest but it is possible to take a train to Markinch and bus from there to Anstruther, from where you can walk along the coast path to Crail or to Pittenweem. Bikes can be booked on the train.

Essence of the place

A string of attractive fishing villages with fine harbours which stretches from Elie to Kingsbarns. You will find beaches, rock pools, sea fishing, boat trips, some good buildings, a museum, cafés, galleries, and coastal walks.

What to see

The cobbled village streets of Pittenweem, Anstruther and Crail all lead down to harbours where the herring fleet once came in. The remaining fishing boats are mostly for shellfish (available in local cafés and restaurants, which include a famous fish and chip shop) but pleasure craft abound and the air still has the tang of salt and seaweed. Anstruther is home to the Scottish Fisheries Museum, part of the National Museums of Scotland, and very well worth visiting. Near to the village is Kellie Castle (National Trust for Scotland), a principally 17th-century building with a fine garden. The Secret Bunker in Redwells Wood was the underground HQ for Scotland during the Cold War. The East Neuk is host to a midsummer festival of music and literature and to a twice-yearly trail of Open Studios that allows you to see work of some 35 local artists. The excellent Pittenweem Arts Festival is held in August.

What to do

Boat trips from Anstruther to the Isle of May are wonderful, particularly for bird lovers during the nesting season. Play golf on an ancient links course at Crail. Take a bike and enjoy Fife Cycleways. Go fossil hunting below the cliffs, especially to see the impressive fossil tree near Crail (see Geology, page 14). The Fife Coastal path provides a well-marked and picturesque trail along the shore from Leven to Crail (21 miles and approximately 11 hours' walking, so best done in stages). Shorter walks abound, many of them sporting good wild flowers during the summer.

ST ANDREWS

Location and transport

It is easy to get there by bus or train, with the added attraction of crossing the Forth Rail Bridge on the way if you're coming from Edinburgh. The nearest station is Leuchars, with frequent buses into town.

Essence of the place

Home of Scotland's oldest university, and its most famous golf course, the town has a wealth of interesting buildings from the castle and cathedral ruins to the colleges and fine town houses, as well as a good harbour and long beaches.

What to see

Wander the three almost parallel main streets and enjoy the university feel of the town centre, with its cafés and bookshops. Notable buildings are St Salvator's chapel, St Leonard's chapel and the quadrangle of what was St Mary's College. Plunge downhill to the harbour, still home to some fishing boats, and strike off to the right to enjoy East Sands, an old fashioned sandy beach. You have to walk further west along The Scores to get to West Sands. On the way you should see the ruins of what must have been a magnificent Romanesque cathedral (you can go up St Rule's Tower) and the splendid castle with its museum. Further on there is miles of open beach where you can really stretch your legs. It is directly below the Royal and Ancient Golf Course (Old Course), so when you return to town, have a look at the formal Victorian buildings, both clubhouse and hotels, that relate to it. St Andrews Aquarium and the university's Botanical Gardens are both good to visit.

What to do

Browse the charity shops for interesting cast-offs of a rather well-heeled student population, and visit the bookshops. Play golf on one of the six courses near the town (probably not the Old Course, which is somewhat exclusive). Further north, at Tentsmuir Forest Trails, ride ponies or go seal watching (see Wildlife, page 41).

DUNDEE

Location and transport

Situated on the north shore of the Firth of Tay, Dundee is easily accessible by train and bus, especially from the Central Belt.

Essence of the place

Scotland's fourth city is enjoying a renaissance. Originally famous for "jute, jam and journalism" as well as being a whaling centre, industry has declined at something like the pace at which tourism has taken over. The students of two universities give the town a young feel, and an enlightened council has done a remarkable job of enlivening the city centre and developing the waterfront into a major attraction.

What to see

No Scottish city boasts more public art. There are installations from a bronze of Desperate Dan of The Dandy (now only available in digital form) in City Square to the much-loved penguins on a church wall nearby. See publicartdundee.org for information on a feast of installations that you can discover on foot. There are art collections in The McManus Galleries and now in the Scottish branch of the V&A. This striking, boatlike building on the shore near to the Tay Bridge is beautifully laid out for viewing art and design treasures. Nearby is the Discovery Centre, where the Dundee-built RSS Discovery has returned as part of a museum. It was the vessel used by Captain Scott on his Antarctic research mission. Further along the shoreline in a corner of the former Victoria Docks is the frigate Unicorn. Built in 1820, she is the oldest warship afloat (a magnet for readers of Hornblower or Patrick O'Brien's nautical novels) and offers an extraordinary glimpse of the hard life of sailors of the time.

What to do

The centre has a good range of shops and cafés. This is a place to explore on foot through the many pedestrianised streets. There are sports centres that offer experience in a variety of sea- and land-based sports, including skiing on the city's dry slope.

STONEHAVEN

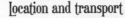

Location and transport

The town is 15 miles south of Aberdeen, easily approached by road, from the A90, and by rail.

Essence of the Place

The former county town of Kincardineshire, it's an Old Red Sandstone (see Geology, page 189) settlement with a fine string of buildings along its half-moon of harbour, long beaches and some attractive streets.

What to see

The old town behind the harbour still has its Tolbooth, now a local museum, and a fine Town House. A mile away is Dunnottar Castle, magnificently sited on the cliffs of a rocky promontory. Its extensive ruins, some of them well preserved, make an exciting visit. If you're looking for a spectacle for Hogmanay, the annual Fireballs Festival makes this a memorable place to experience the dying hours of the old year, and welcome in the new.

What to do

Take a bracing walk along the sand and shingle beaches and retreat to a café as the wind off the North Sea can be keen! You can also take a walk to Dunnottar (2 miles) and enjoy the ORS cliffs. On a warm day try out the open air swimming pool, followed up by an ice cream

from Aunty Betty's. Visit the RSPB reserve at Fowlsheugh to see puffins and other seabirds nesting – including guillemots, kittiwakes and fulmars. Play golf on the local course or take a boat trip along the coast and get an impressive view of Dunnottar from the sea.

FINDHORN

Location and transport

About 30 miles east of Inverness, Findhorn is on the coast of Moray Firth, four miles north of Forres on the A96. Easiest to reach by car, but buses (Stagecoach 31, 31B) are available, and there's a station at Forres.

Essence of the place

A sea lagoon, Findhorn Bay; Scotland's largest 'intentional community', the Findhorn Foundation; an old fishing village; and a long shingle beach make up this unusual place.

What to see

Enjoy Findhorn Bay, fringed with pine trees, before turning into the discreetly hidden Findhorn Foundation (see Culture, page 140). Visit the community's shop with local and organic food and crafts. Wander the site to see the eco-village, consisting of both large private houses, and smaller, more affordable homes. The Universal Hall is an interesting building with a good café, that hosts courses, conventions, meetings and world-class concerts. The community's gardens are also worth a visit. Further along the public road is Findhorn itself, an attractive former fishing village with an old pub and the Royal Findhorn Yacht Club. To the east of the village runs a seven-mile stretch of beach round Burghead Bay, good for birdwatching and for dune and shingle flowers (see Plants, pp 51 and 54).

What to do

A circular walk around the peninsula can take in all the features. Starting at the eco-village, head for Burghead Bay and turn west towards the old village, returning by the shore of Findhorn Bay. Take a boat trip to see dolphins. Visit Culbin Forest and Sands, a few miles to the west, for safe and easy family cycling and rich wildlife (see Plants, pp 212 and 55).

THE BLACK ISLE

Location and transport

Scattered sites make a car easiest for seeing this peninsula on the north shore of the Moray Firth, to the north of Inverness. A bus service to Cromarty via Fortrose runs approximately hourly (Stagecoach 26). It's relatively flat, so has easy cycling.

Essence of the place

A low-lying, fertile peninsula with a warm microclimate and some interesting villages. Dolphins near Rosemarkie and the beautifully laid-out 18th-century town of Cromarty are top attractions.

What to see

Glance at the Clootie Well in Munlochy or visit the Black Isle Brewery for organic beer before travelling to Fortrose for the turn-off to Chanonry Point. Here, at the right stage of the tide, dolphins can reliably be seen leaping only a few metres off-shore (see Wildlife, page 40). Drive on to Cromarty and abandon the car to discover the whole of this attractive town on foot. It is a mixture of small cottages and more substantial and well-built houses, many of them dating to about 1770. Hugh Miller's birthplace (now a museum) and an Institute bearing his name are there. Walk through a tunnel below Cromarty House to see the attractive graveyard with a memorial to Hugh Miller's 17-month-old daughter – said to be the last stone he cut. There are good cafés, pubs, an excellent cheese shop, antique shops, a bookshop, and a pleasing church. The old quays and jetties are a constant reminder of Cromarty's past as a port for ferries and North Sea trade.

What to do

Take a boat trip from Cromarty to see dolphins, seals and seabirds. There are forest walks at Ord Hill and several golf courses in the area. Walk from Cromarty to see a natural arch, McFarquhar's Bed, and beyond, to Eathie, where there is good fossil hunting but watch the tide! Walking from Rosemarkie out to Chanonry Point and back will reward you with a nice wee harbour and a good sand and shingle beach.

GOLSPIE AND THE EAST COAST OF SUTHERLAND AND CAITHNESS

Location and transport
On the A9, north of Inverness, Golspie, Brora and Helmsdale have stations with regular trains running from Inverness to Wick and Thurso.

Essence of the place
Golspie is a village expanded by the Duke of Sutherland in the 19th century to house tenants cleared for sheep, with a formal grid of streets and a small fishing harbour. The coast north of here has a special quality of light and interesting topography.

What to see
Dunrobin Castle, one mile north of Golspie, was the seat of the Dukes of Sutherland, and an encapsulation of their wealth and influence. Originally a 14th-century castle, Dunrobin was remodelled during the 19th century in the Scottish Baronial style, with fairy-tale turrets, good displays (especially the seamstress's shop) and lovely gardens. Look up at the 100-foot-high statue of the duke above Golspie village, or walk up and relish the irony of the plinth that praises him as a good landlord: he and Elizabeth, his duchess, were generally loathed. Have a walk on the beach here and warm up in a café or hotel. At the other end of the town visit the excellent geology and fossil museum, the Orcadian Stone Exhibition. Travelling north, you will pass Golspie Mill, producing stone-ground, organic meals and flours. It's not open to the public but look out for its first-rate products in local shops. Further north the road rises and falls, giving superb views of the North Sea, silvery and shimmering on a sunny day. At Helmsdale stop off at Timespan Museum and Arts Centre (open most of the year, with a good café) to learn about the local gold rush and find out more about the history of the area from Viking times. Further north, visit the Dunbeath Heritage Centre (open most of the year) to discover something of the life of Neil Gunn, one of Scotland's great writers.

What to do
Beach walks, cliff walks (in the early summer alive with nesting seabirds – see Wildlife, page 48) and a delightful trail up Neil Gunn's Strath at Dunbeath are all good. Golf is available at some of Scotland's finest courses. The Big Burn Walk at Dunrobin boasts diverse local flora.

THURSO

Location and transport

The most northerly town in Scotland, at the end (or beginning!) of the A9, and the terminus of the rail line, Thurso's port, Scrabster, is the departure point for the Orkney ferry.

Essence of the place

A planned Georgian town with fine formal streets and some good buildings, an attractive shore with beaches, a castle, and a working port, it is now a centre for surfing.

What to see

Enjoy the wide, and usually quiet, streets and home in on Old St Peter's Church, about the only building surviving from the medieval port, and the public library which is neo-classical. Housed in the former town hall is Caithness Horizons, an excellent museum with a gallery and café. It tells the story of the area from geological times to the development of Dounreay Nuclear research establishment in the 20th century. Also celebrated is Sir John Sinclair, who was responsible not only for the remodelling of the town in the late 18th and early 19th centuries but also for the First Statistical Accounts, which give us invaluable information about every parish in Scotland at that time. Twelve miles east is the Castle of May, home of the late Queen Mother, with good gardens. Further east is Dunnet Head, less famous than John O'Groats but actually the most northerly point on the mainland of Britain – and it feels like it! Both are worth visiting, the latter for the sight of the lighthouse, the fine cliffs and the stacks at Duncansby Head (see Geology, page 23).

What to do

Walk from Thurso to Scrabster to see if any interesting fish have been landed and to take a turn on the beach, or walk out to Thurso Castle. If you are brave, experienced, and hardy, join the hundreds who now come here for the surfing in the bay, where the rocky reefs concentrate the power of the Atlantic to make it one of the best locations in the world for the sport. You can play golf in Thurso and at Reay, or if it's cold and wet you can go to the cinema.

BETTYHILL, TONGUE AND DURNESS

Location and transport

West of Thurso, on a small and winding road, you need a car, or a bike if you are resilient enough to cope with wind, to explore the coast and villages.

Essence of the place

The coast is wildly rugged, with a dramatic backdrop of mountains, and the villages small and little visited. Bettyhill is attractive and scattered, Tongue more concentrated, with hotels and a hostel. Durness has a splendid beach and interesting geology.

What to see

It's tempting just to drive on and on along the mostly single-track road but stop off to see Strathy Bay, backed by sand dunes that are rich in wild flowers, and set around with good rock formations and caves. At the Strathnaver Museum in Bettyhill, housed in the 18th-century church, you can learn more about the Norse and Gaelic past, the Clearances and emigration. Tongue is spectacularly situated above a kyle of that name. Walk to the small tower on the causeway below the House of Tongue and to the castle ruins at Caisteal Bharraigh. In Durness, make for the beach and enjoy a windblown walk, whatever the weather.

What to do

You can join a pony trek from Bettyhill along the Torrisdale beach or explore the good dunes there, looking for wild flowers. Master the geology of the Moine Thrust at Durness, where its edge is visible (see Geology, page 26). The short walk at A'craobh, approached from the Borgie Forest car park, is a spiral woodland path displaying the Gaelic Tree Alphabet. Don't turn south from Tongue but drive on and round to Blairmore, near Kinlochbervie, the parking place for the five-mile walk to Sandwood Bay. This is said to be the most magnificent beach in Scotland. You will walk through botanically rich machair at Sheigra, a system of dunes (see Plants, pages 58 and 51), and some large areas of wind-eroded peatland, rich in wildlife, before you get to the huge area of sand. Take your binoculars!

LOCHINVER

Location and transport

Take the A837 through Assynt, or follow the small coast road from south of Unapool that winds through Lochinver on its way to Achiltibue. You can catch the bus from Ullapool (Scotbus 809 & Stagecoach 167).

Essence of the place

Assynt's wonderful wild country, of silver rock, forest and mountain run through with lochs and pools, terminates in a neat fishing village with harbour, hotels, cafés and shops including a chandler and a butcher – important in this remote area.

What to see

There is just one main street, which has cafés (including Lochinver Larder, the well-known pie shop) and hotels. From it you can look south-east to Suilven's great rock, bursting from the coastal plain. The loch makes a natural harbour, still with some fishing boats. Visit Highland Stoneware or the craft potter at Glencanisp. There's an Iron Age roundhouse built on a rock above the pink sands of Stoer beach, which is most easily approached from Clachtoll beach car park. Don't miss the spectacular white sands of Achmelvich beach and the area of machair behind it.

What to do

Walk through Culag Community Woods (to the north of the village) to the sparkling White Shore pebble beach and ascend to the lookout point from where you get one of the very best views of Suilven. Walk the highly indented coast from Achmelvich to Altnabradhan through the Lewisian Gneiss landscape, enjoying the splendid flora. On a good day swim, go sea kayaking, sea fishing, or head inland to climb Suilven, Canisp, Cul Mor or Cul Beg, all of which belong to the local community. This is a good area for foraging, with seaweeds and maritime plants and for seeing seabirds and mammals: otters, harbour seals, herons, Arctic terns and many more.

ULLAPOOL

Location and transport

Located on the A 835 on the north side of Loch Broom, it's easiest by car, although there are limited bus services (and the ferry from Stornoway).

Essence of the place

A planned fishing settlement of white houses, prettily strung along a shore with a port at the further end. It has a feel of a holiday town but is still the regional economic centre.

What to see

Explore the three main streets that lie one above another on the hillside. The furthest back is wide and generous, with gardens. The Ullapool Museum and Visitor Centre, packed with artefacts and interest is near here. The lower streets have a good array of pleasant cafés and pubs and some interesting shops including a bookshop at the renowned Ceilidh Place. Walk down to the port, which is the ferry terminal for Stornoway, and the home of smaller cruise boats as well as a fishing fleet. Tall ships, or even a Viking ship replica occasionally moor here. Drive north to Knockan Crag for an amazing panorama of the distinctive helmet-shaped hills of Sutherland and an informative geological trail. Continue north and take the turning to Achiltibuie, past Stac Pollaidh (a quick but quite strenuous climb). From the linear village with pubs and a shop you can take a ferry to the Summer Isles. Drive south to visit Leckmelm Shrubbery and Arboretum, or walk there on the track above the road and through the woods. A little further south is the Corrieshalloch Gorge, an impressive chasm that can be viewed from a bridge.

What to do

Sea fishing, sea cruises, birdwatching, some water sports, and golf are all available in Ullapool. There is a swimming pool and gym. Climb An Teallach to experience the ancient rock of Torridon sandstone topped with Cambrian quartzite (see Geology, page 26).

GAIRLOCH, POOLEWE AND AREA

Location and transport

Both villages are on the A832 and only easily accessible by car.

Essence of the place

Gairloch is a particularly attractive Highland village with sandy beaches, rocky shores and good mountain scenery. Poolewe is another lovely village and the home of a spectacular garden.

What to see

Inverewe Gardens (National Trust for Scotland) are an essential visit. Osgood Mackenzie developed them in the late 19th century, making use of shelter-belts and the mild influence of the Gulf Stream to grow exotic plants. The village of Poolewe has a café and gallery and a pretty main street. Gairloch is equally attractive. In addition to a shop and hotel, it boasts sandy beaches on which to stroll, rock pools, and superb views. Gairloch Heritage Museum will give you more information about the area and its Iron Age and Viking history.

What to do

You can take a whole range of walks, varying from one-hour strolls at sea level to serious ascents on nearby mountains. The short walks around Flowerdale are particularly pleasant. Cruise in a glass-bottomed boat from Gairloch to see the magnificent marine world below the surface or take a boat that goes further out to see dolphins and larger wildlife. Pony trekking and golf are also on offer. If you want a car trip, visit Loch Maree with its picturesque pine and oak forest and drive on, turning west at Kinlochewe to enjoy Beinn Eighe with its outstanding, steep, rocky trail and the amazing Torridon landscape (see Geology, page 26).

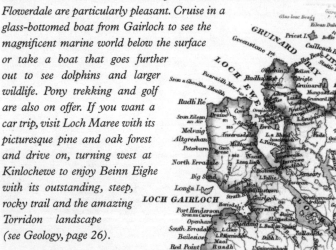

APPLECROSS

Location and transport

The peninsula is on a loop road, which leaves the A896 at Tornapress, just beyond Lochcarron, and rejoins it at Shieldaig. The stretch between there and Applecross village includes the very high Pass of the Cattle (Bealach na Bà), which has terrific views but is terrifying to drive in bad weather. The pass is something of a mecca for experienced road-climbing cyclists who thrive on extreme challenge – and have nerves of steel. The nearest train station is at Strathcarron, from where there's a limited bus service.

Essence of the place

A remote and rugged place with wonderful views across to Skye and a charming village, beach, inn, and a good café in a walled garden.

What to see

Enjoy all the scenery. Visit the Heritage Centre and get the maps to show you walks around the Applecross estate's forests, along the river, and through former crofting townships. The walled garden offers a sheltered place to explore, and there's a good café. The inn has excellent food and live music. Both the inn and the village shop sell His Bloody Project, by Graeme Macrae Burnet, a bestselling novel shortlisted for the Booker Prize in 2016, that is set in 19th-century Culduie, a hamlet nearby.

What to do

Paddle and muck about on the beaches. Explore the full length of the wee road that runs south from Applecross Estate to Toscaig, where fishing still goes on. This was the end point of the Parliamentary road over the Pass of the Cattle, built in 1822. Bring along binoculars for spotting seabirds and seals. You might see a golden eagle.

PLOCKTON

Location and transport

On a loop road from the A87, north of Kyle of Lochalsh. Accessible by bus and train (station near the village) and a good place for cycling.

Essence of the place

An attractive arc of nicely painted houses, with shops, cafés, galleries and palm trees makes a picturesque waterfront to a quiet arm of Loch Carron.

What to see

Walk the causeway to the little tidal island, a tiny distance but enjoyed by children. Explore the street and read up about its history as a fishing settlement created by the local laird to accommodate some of those he turned from the land during the Clearances. See whether the village hall is showing an exhibition. Take the brae walk along the loch to Duncraig Castle. Visit Stromeferry for the famous "Strome Ferry (no ferry)" sign!

What to do

Go seal watching or fishing by boat. Craig Rare Breeds Farm is a mile or two east, and makes an excellent outing for children who will see native breeds of poultry and farm animals, as well as llamas and peacocks on a walk that leads down to a series of beaches the other side of the railway. Lochalsh Woodland Garden is a few miles south and near it the Bright Water Visitor Centre where you can learn about Gavin Maxwell (see Wildlife, page 32), otters and other wildlife.

ARISAIG

Location and transport
Just off the A830 between Fort William and Mallaig, served by buses and trains.

Essence of the place

A series of sparkling beaches behind dunes, connected by the old Road to the Isles: a romantic and delightful place. Scenes from the movie Local Hero *were filmed in Arisaig, near the beach at the campsite at Camusdarach.*

What to see
Stop off on the shore of Loch nan Uamh, south of Arisaig, and walk out to the Prince's Cairn, which marks Bonnie Prince Charlie's departure point from Scotland to France in 1746. Wander the long stretches of the Sands of Morar, which have not been ruined by camping and caravans, although they are frequented, and held dear, by thousands of people. Arisaig village has a shop, cafés and an excellent, upmarket restaurant with comfortable accommodation. The Arisaig area was used during the Second World War as a base to train agents for missions in Nazi-controlled Europe. Visit the Lands, Sea and Islands Centre in the heart of the village to find out more, and to see displays on local history, flora and fauna. Travel the short distance north to the 19th-century fishing port of Mallaig and visit the heritage centre by the railway station. From Mallaig, you can take the ferry to Skye, or a day trip by boat to Inverie in Knoydart, the most remote part of the UK mainland.

What to do
Walk, swim, cycle, kayak, or play golf. Take a boat trip to Eigg or Rum, or join a wildlife cruise for potential sightings of whales, dolphins, seals, sharks, otters and seabirds, including golden eagles and sea eagles.

SALEN, STRONTIAN AND SUNART

Location and transport

On the A861 and most easily accessible via the Corran ferry and through Glen Tarbert. A car is best for this remote area but buses do run from Fort William.

Essence of the place

The oakwoods of Sunart are a magnificent relic of ancient Atlantic rainforest. Strontian is mostly a 1970s village but with an interesting mining history.

What to see

Ariundle National Nature Reserve is the best place to park and walk in the oakwoods. Look at the rich crusts of mosses, lichen, liverworts and ferns carried by the trees (see Plants, page 61) and watch for the level platforms that betray old charcoal burning sites. Visit the Ariundle Centre for its craft shop, café and local information. Strontian village was an early 18th-century lead mining centre and gave its name to the element strontium.

What to do

Hire a boat and go sailing, kayaking, canoeing or fishing on Loch Sunart. Take the long drive to Ardnamurchan Point and lighthouse, the most westerly point of mainland Britain. The road threads along one of Scotland's most beautiful shores to Kilchoan (ferry to Mull) and Mingary Castle, before turning north and inland to cross the peninsula. From Salen you can head north to seek out the remarkable vitrified fort above Shielfoot, although you will need an OS map to find it.

ARDFERN

Location and transport

Off the A816 south of Oban. West Coast Motors operates a regular bus service (423) from Oban to Lochgilphead that serves this and other villages.

Essence of the place

A dreamy, sheltered loch and marina with a wilder coast just a walk away over the peninsula, Ardfern is near to the exceptional valley and museum at Kilmartin, full of archaeological treasures.

What to see

Explore the Craignish peninsula on foot, seeing the striking rock forms, and ruined chapel with good medieval grave slabs. You can walk on to Aird where you can often hear the Corryvreckan whirlpool. Travel south to Kilmartin, enjoying the views of the green valley full of ancient sites from Neolithic cup-and-ring marks to Medieval remains. It stretches from Carnasserie Castle at the north, to Dunadd, the hill-top centre of the Dark Age Kingdom of Dalriada, at its southern end. Kilmartin church has splendid Medieval grave slabs and is next door to Kilmartin House Museum, an outpost of civilisation and excellence. Its café, bookshop, video introduction, intelligent archaeological displays and the care put into good design and local provenance of materials are not to be missed. Ask to see the remarkable library, constructed by hand entirely from local woods.

What to do

Take a boat trip to see the Corryvreckan, with plenty of wildlife en route in the Sounds of Jura, or hire a sailing boat and join the yachties.

CAMPBELTOWN, CARRADALE AND THE KINTYRE PENINSULA

Location and transport

You will need a car or bike. There is a ferry from Ardrossan to Campbeltown, after which you can potter up the east side of the Mull of Kintyre on the B842. An alternative is to drive the A83 all the way down the peninsula, with lovely views westwards across the beaches of Islay, Jura and Gigha.

Essence of the place

Campbeltown is a port and a prospering town, with all facilities; Carradale a quiet village, visited for its beaches, harbour, archaeology, medieval stone carvings, and heritage centres.

What to see

The town is not an obvious seaside resort but there are plenty of things to see and do such as galleries, a museum, and a heritage centre. Six miles away, on the west coast, is the beautifully sited Machrihanish Seabird and Wildlife Observatory and spectacular sandy beaches. At Southend there is a golf course and at the Mull of Kintyre a lighthouse, where seals can be heard calling on the rocky shore, a variety of unusual seabirds breed. As you move north up the east coast, you will come across a string of things to visit. Saddell Abbey, with fine medieval carvings, and Castle (the latter not open to the public) are worth seeing, as is the vitrified fort on Carradale Point. Here you can ponder on the great unsolved mystery of Scottish Iron Age archaeology: how and why was the fort vitrified? The village, beach, café, and heritage centre nearby are all worth a visit. On the beaches, admire the remarkable, folded rock formations.

What to do

Fishing trips, sea tours round Gigha and Arran (for more on Arran, see pages 180–82), surfing, mountain biking, cycling, sailing, cinema, swimming, riding, leisure centre, diving, golf (choice of six courses) and wildlife watching.

DUNOON

Location and transport

The town lies to the east of the Cowal peninsula, on the west shore of the Firth of Clyde. It is a traditional day out from Glasgow, and until recently you could still go 'Doon the Watter' from Greenock (accessible by train) in the paddle steamer Waverley. The splendid old boat has been restored, and there is also still a foot passenger ferry from Greenock, and a car ferry from McInroy's Point. The West Coast Motors 486 bus gives access from Inveraray and Glasgow.

Essence of the place

The town is period piece. It was largely built in the second quarter of the 19th century, when steam power brought the rich of Glasgow to build villas in this attractive watering place, with its backdrop of the mountains of Cowal. Very soon many more holidaymakers came in their thousands, with buckets and spades, to enjoy traditional seaside delights.

What to see

Take in the grand Regency and early Victorian villas along the shore and the even grander hotels in the town, particularly the Argyll, which overlooks the recently (and beautifully) restored pier. The town's founder, James Ewing, MP, built Dunoon Castle House out of the remains of a medieval castle, and it is now the town's museum. Only seven miles away is the Royal Botanic Garden Benmore, which features many magnificent trees, including an avenue of giant redwoods.

What to do

Outdoor pursuits: walks, hill walking, running, mountain biking, golfing, sailing and kayaking are available. There are waymarked trails in an area known as Bishop's Glen, and nearer to Benmore, in beautiful Puck's Glen. If you stay in the town you can play crazy golf near the sea or seek out one of the numerous cafés. If you have a car, you can explore a whole series of sites which reveal the early Christian history of Cowal, some of which pre-date St Columba. See www.faithincowal.org.

AYR

Location and transport
Off the A77 around 30 miles south of Glasgow and served by all forms of transport.

Essence of the place
A town with a strong sense of history, some good buildings and bridges, still a working port with an important harbour, but also a seaside resort with beaches.

What to see
See Auld Ayr Toun with its 15th-century stone bridge; the old pubs; Loudoun Hall, a merchant's house built in 1513; Cromwell's Citadel, from where he governed a good deal of Scotland; the Town Hall with its tall, Renaissance-style spire; the Robert Burns Birthplace Museum; the McKechnie Institute; Rozelle House and Maclaurin Gallery exhibitions of contemporary Scottish art; the remaining riverside wharves which once handled tobacco, sugar and salt; and the beaches. It's also well worth visiting the impressive Culzean Castle a few miles to the south. There, as well as enjoying the historic

building, you can have coastal walks and look out to sea towards Ailsa Craig, the great rock that lies off the Ayrshire coast.

What to do
Go to the races. Walk the 'Lang Scots Mile'. Take a boat trip from Girvan to Ailsa Craig.

PORTPATRICK

Location and transport

On the very end of the A77 and the midpoint of the west coast of the Rhinns of Galloway. Stranraer (six miles away) has a station and there are hourly buses (Service 367). You can also walk there on the Southern Upland Way.

Essence of the place

A very pretty village of painted houses lined up round a picturesque harbour, set within a cleft in steep cliffs and with a sandy beach.

What to see

The former ferry port to Ireland, abandoned in the 19th century because it was too exposed, Portpatrick has since been a minor tourist resort with cafés, shops, a pottery, cliff-top viewpoints, a small lighthouse, and Dunskey Castle and Glen, which is a short walk away along a cliff path. The point where the Southern Upland Way starts (for most people, but ends for a hardy few who walk against the prevailing wind!) is a good viewing spot. The first stretch of this 212-mile-long coast to coast path makes a longer walk, which can easily be turned into a circular route.

What to do

Walk, take a boat trip to explore the Solway coast, or cross the Rhinns peninsula to reach Luce Sands. Stop at Killantringan beach (descending carefully down the access path) for a beautiful cove and rockpooling, although swimming is hazardous because of the currents. There is a folk festival in Portpatrick each September. Travel south to the Mull of Galloway, calling at Logan Botanic Garden. The far end of the peninsula is a very good place to watch for whales, dolphins and basking sharks (see Wildlife, page 38).

WIGTOWN AND THE MACHARS

Location and transport

On the A714, six miles south of its junction with the A75 to Stranraer. You will need a car or bike as the nearest bus stop is miles away in Newton Stewart.

Essence of the place

Since becoming Scotland's 'Book Town' (see Culture, page 135), Wigtown's central square and red sandstone streets have seen a great resurgence with many bookshops, cafés and pleasant short walks.

What to see

Browse the remarkable second-hand bookshops and be sure to visit the newly cleaned Town Hall with its museum and Wildlife Viewing Room, which has a webcam feed from a nearby osprey nest. Walk the circular route that passes the ruins of the old parish church and the Martyrs' Memorial, commemorating the horrible death of two Covenanters who were staked out to drown with the rising tide. The seashore is a muddy estuary but quite botanically rich (see Plants, page 65) and good for other wildlife.

Wigtown used to be a port, but the River Bladnoch has silted up and the harbour is no longer usable. The triangular peninsula of the Machars is not machair in the Hebridean sense, but low-lying fertile land. Top attractions are Whithorn, for its historic church and abbey ruins and pretty village street, and the Isle of Whithorn, for St Ninian's Church, perched on a cliff facing Ireland, from whence the saint originally came. Further round the peninsula you can park and take the walk through lanes to a stony shore and St Ninian's Cave.

What to do

Visit the annual book festival in October for world-class talks and other cultural life. Take local walks, many of them waymarked. Further afield, walk to see Bruce's Stone, or mountain bike in Glentrool, north of Newton Stewart or wander in the almost adjacent Wood of Cree nature reserve. If you are lucky with a clear night, experience the local dark skies at Galloway Astronomy Centre.

KIRCUDBRIGHT

Location and transport

On the A711, (off the A75) south west of Dumfries, between Castle Douglas and Gatehouse of Fleet. Car or bike are the only real options.

Essence of the place

One of the most attractive towns in Scotland, considered to be an artists' place and still home to many of them, with picturesque streets, a waterfront, a harbour, and good cafés and shops.

What to see

A fine 18th-century town house, Broughton House, was home of the artist E.A. Hornel, well known from the 1880s onwards as one of the 'Glasgow Boys'. Both the house and its attractive garden are open to the public. MacLellan's Castle is a tall and eye-catching ruin, built after it had a real defensive purpose, although the town's walls saw active service in keeping out the English in 1560, only 20 years after they were built. Visit the local art galleries selling contemporary work, especially during the annual Spring Fling, when Dumfries and Galloway has a weekend of Open Studios. Don't neglect the fine old pubs, several of them serving excellent food. The waterfront is more river and estuary than seaside since Kirkudbright Bay silted up but is still pleasant to stroll along, especially when the tide is running in.

What to do

Visit Sandyhills (south of Dalbeattie) with this book in hand and read Ronald Turnbull's account of the geology: how greywacke and the Needle's Eye sea arch formed. Visit Galloway Wildlife Conservation Park near the town to see European mammals such as lynx. Drive north to visit moated Threave Castle. Play golf on the town course.

A Handbook of Scotland's Coasts

SPORTING DAYS OUT: CYCLING

There are wonderful cycle routes for all abilities around our coastlines, and if you're on a traffic-free route and can look about you, you'll see so much more from the saddle than you would travelling by other means. We've suggested a few destinations in our Days Out itineraries and below, but the possibilities are almost endless. The National Cycle Network consists of routes that are relatively quiet and cyclist-friendly. Sustrans also offers safety information, cycling tips and a wealth of route suggestions, both for road cycling and off-road cycling around Scotland. For more information on the routes we've highlighted here, visit the Sustrans website.

Easy and medium rides

Ayrshire Coast: *19-miles along National Cycle Network Route 7 from Irvine to Ayr: views across to Arran and a train back to the start.*

Bervie Bay: *A 4½-mile trip from Johnshaven to Inverbervie, along a farm track and disused railway, which offers great views of the North Sea.*

Black Isle Biking: *Visit www.transitionblackisle.org for information on scenic coastal cycle routes linking Cromarty, Fortrose and Dingwall, and on to Alness and Tain.*

A Bute of a Route: *A stunning 32-mile circular route around the Cowal Peninsula from Tighnabruaich, with views toward Bute. (For more about Bute, see pages 178–79 in the Islands chapter.)*

Great Cumbrae Loop: *An easy, mainly flat 9-mile circular island ride following the coast road, starting from the ferry terminal.*

Moray Miles: *Follow a 26-mile coastal stretch of the National Cycle Network's mammoth Route 1 between Banff and Spey Bay. The route offers fantastic wildlife-watching possibilities.*

Longer and more challenging rides

There are long routes available around all of Scotland's coastlines. *For deserted beaches and long stretches with little or no traffic, try the Western Isles chain NCN Route 780. For a more challenging ride, try a circular route in Assynt, from Achiltibuie or Lochinver. The hardest route is the Bealach na Bà on the Applecross peninsula. For experts only!*

TAKING TO THE WATER

WILD SWIMMING

Swimming safely in the wild is all about knowledge and experience: knowing your limits, taking account of the conditions (especially currents and tides, which can be ferocious and unpredictable even to those who know a coastline well, and weather too), and finding the best location.

To begin safely, join a club or a training course, and always stick to known, safe river bathing spots or sheltered lochans – or in a lido. For your first swims in the open sea, try a lifeguarded beach (you can find your nearest lifeguarded beach on the RNLI's website, rnli.org). Certainly don't risk swimming alone, even if you consider yourself a strong swimmer. It's simply too dangerous. Apart from the currents and tides, it's all too easy to become incapacitated in cold water, even when wearing a wetsuit and in relatively mild conditions, and there are other hazards. You could find yourself tangled in seaweed or hurt on concealed rocks.

If you've only ever swum in a pool it's hard to convey just how different swimming in the wild can be!   FI MARTYNOGA

COASTAL ROWING

Coastal rowing has taken off in the last few years. In 2009 the Scottish Fisheries Museum at Anstruther commissioned Iain Oughtred, a Skye-based boat designer, to draw up plans for a boat based on a Fair Isle skiff. The result was the St Ayles skiff – a 22-foot rowing boat with a hint of Norse influence. Vessels are made in kit form, which ensures that their size and weight remain fairly even. As the boats are available at a relatively affordable price, the idea took off quickly. From an initial regatta in 2010 that had just six boats, there are now clubs all round the Scottish coast (see Portobello, page 186), a growing number in England and abroad. The skiff is designed for four rowers and a cox, but takes a larger team of volunteers to construct. There is no need for specialist knowledge, and age is not a barrier: teenagers and pensioners work side by side.

Aboard, rowers discover the joy of making their skiff sweep through the water and ride purposefully against the waves. Races of varying distances are now frequent events. But many people derive equal pleasure by simply rowing offshore to view their own coastline from a new angle, or by travelling to another club, to see theirs. The skiffs are light enough to be lifted on and off trailers and launched by their own crew, so they're a great new way to explore the Scottish coastline.   FI MARTYNOGA

SEA KAYAKING

From a smooth and silent glide over mirror-calm waters to a roaring thrill ride in tempestuous tidal rapids, sea kayaking in Scotland has something for everyone. The north boasts cliffs, towering sea stacks, and caves. The east has long, sandy beaches, rolling surf and amazing bird colonies. If it's variety you seek, look no further than the west coast.

Oban is a great base to start from. Sea kayaks are available to hire, with the option of a guide for beginners. Ferries provide easy access to islands, including Mull, Lismore, Coll and Tiree, and kayaks are carried free of charge. Seals, dolphins, whales, even basking sharks have all been spotted by kayakers off Oban's coastline.

Even on calm days, the right gear is a must. A buoyancy aid, a spraydeck, map, pump and a spare paddle are all essentials, as well as warm and waterproof layers. If the weather is kind, these can be stored in the hatches of the kayak. There is no shortage of space in a sea kayak, so take plenty of equipment, and be sure you know how to use it. Tuition is available from many excellent providers around Scotland. CHRIS WITHERS

SURFING

Surfing in northern Scotland isn't just about the thrill of riding a constantly moving and changing mound of water – it's about the vast, expansive beaches of Caithness and Sutherland; the thrill of that first glimpse of the ocean; the trek to a remote beach; the powerful, awe-inspiring ocean. The water will be crystal-clear and there may be seals to chat to, or dolphins playing offshore. You have to know this highly dynamic coastline well if you want to find good waves. There are so many variables of tide, wind direction and daylight, especially in the winter months. You may find 50mph winds driving hail into your eyes. You lose feeling in your hands and feet and shiver uncontrollably as you try to change out of your 6mm wetsuit, hood, boots and gloves with numb fingers. [Don't take risks with being too cold! (ed)] Then you laugh it off with a friend and a pint of Guinness by the fire of a local pub.

The epicentre of Scottish surfing is Thurso. The best surf is in colder temperatures. You can still get lessons and hire equipment from the local surf school. The "Thurso East" wave, with the repetitive, predictable way it breaks, it is very popular. Advanced surfers: study tides and weather forecasts and take a look west: you may find a deserted beach.

DAVID GARETH THOMAS

About the Contributors

Jim Crumley is a nature writer, journalist, broadcaster and poet with more than thirty books to his name. Jim's most recent books form a tetralogy charting the seasons and climate change in Scotland, and previous titles focus on species reintroductions, including on beavers and sea eagles. *The Nature of Autumn* was shortlisted for a Wainwright award (2017) and he has also been shortlisted for a Saltire Society literary award.

Michael Kerrigan is an Edinburgh-based writer, historian and critic. The author of more than thirty books on history and culture, including the companion title *A Handbook of Scotland's History*, he is a long-standing critic for the *Scotsman* and the *London Review of Books*.

Chris and Margaret Knowles, a retired archaeologist and a retired teacher, have been part of many National Trust for Scotland work parties on St Kilda and have often led excavations and site recording there.

Fi Martynoga is an environmental activist, journalist, researcher, and a renowned figure in Scottish nature, history, sustainability and food circles. She has several widely praised books to her name, and has edited and contributed to the companion titles in this series, *A Handbook of Scotland's Wild Harvests* and *A Handbook of Scotland's Trees*.

Ian Stephen is a writer, storyteller, artist and sailor from the Isle of Lewis. His prose, poetry and drama have been published around the world.

David Gareth Thomas, originally from Newcastle, moved to the Black Isle in 1990 when he was 18 and was new to surfing. He has been building his skills and his enthusiasm ever since.

Ronald Turnbull is a geographer and a walker. The author of more than a dozen highly regarded walking books and guides, he has won four awards from the Outdoor Writers and Photographers Guild, including Best Outdoor Book for *Granite and Grit*, a walker's guide to geology.

Andy Wightman MSP has been a Scottish Green MSP for the Lothian region since 2016 and is an influential campaigner, writer and researcher who is best known for his work on land use, land ownership, fiscal reform and local democracy in Scotland. He is the author of *Who Owns Scotland* and *The Poor Had No Lawyers*.

Chris Withers As a freelance outdoor instructor, Chris works and plays both on the sea in his kayak, and in the mountains all over Scotland, and can be found doing so in all weathers.

Acknowledgements & Further Reading

The editor would like to thank Greg Kenicer and Crinan Alexander for checking the veracity of the plant chapter, in particular the Latin names; Kate and Iain McEwan for recommending the best textbooks for the Coastal Bounty chapter, and putting me in touch with Janet Ullman of the Highland Biodiversity Project, which is an excellent source of information about the wildlife of Scotland's coasts. It was she who recommended Roddy Maclean to me, and it is to Roddy that we owe all the Gaelic names for plants and sea creatures. He assiduously read and commented on the Coastal Bounty chapter, improving it greatly in the process. Many people checked the Days Out entries: Lizzie Findlay, Ronald Turnbull, Sam Wade, Innes Miller, Mandy Haggith, Kate Roberts are to be thanked in particular, and many others, too numerous to name, who made useful suggestions. The publisher would also like to thank Craig Hillsley, Jenny Hamrick and Sophie Franklin for editorial assistance, and to acknowledge the late (and great) Jo Morley, who laid out the first edition of this book and did the picture research. For image credits in the first section of colour photographs, please see the copyright page.

Further reading & species identification

Houston, Fiona and Milne, Xa, *Seaweed and Eat It*. London, Virgin Books, 2008.

Keble Martin, W., *The Concise British Flora in Colour*. London, Ebury Press and Michael Joseph, 1965 (and later editions which will have more up-to-date taxonomy).

Plass, Maya, *RSPB Handbook of the Seashore*. London, Bloomsbury, 2013.

Polunin, Oleg, *Collins Photoguide to Wild Flowers of Britain and Northern Europe*. Collins, 1988.

Preston-Mafham, Rod & Ken, *Seashore* (Collins Gem series). London, HarperCollins, 2004 edition.

Rose, Francis, *The Wild Flower Key*. London, Frederick Warne, 1981.

Stace, Clive, *New Flora of the British Isles*, 3rd edition. Cambridge University Press, 2010.

Wells, Emma, *A Field Guide to British Seaweeds*, Environment Agency, 2009.

Wright, John, *Edible Seashore* (River Cottage Handbook series). London, Bloomsbury, 2009.

www.nhm.ac.uk/nature-online/british-natural-history/seaweeds-survey/identify-seaweeds/index.html

Index

Index

Index

ALSO AVAILABLE

Companion titles on Scotland's natural heritage

A Handbook of Scotland's Wild Harvests

This inspirational guide is packed with invaluable know-how on Scotland's wild harvest, covering what, where, when and how you can use your bounty in sustainable ways – from the most useful and widespread of species to the less well-known, and from leaves and berries to saps, seeds, seaweeds, mosses and wood. Learn how to begin or extend a repertoire of wild foods as well as materials that can be used as dyes, remedies, and around the home.

"This incredibly informative handbook details all things edible, drinkable, sustainable." NEIL FORBES, CHEF OF THE YEAR 2014

Fi Martynoga, ed • £12.99 • Revised ed. ISBN: 9781910192184

A Handbook of Scotland's Trees

A concise, comprehensive handbook, compiled by Fi Martynoga and fellow Reforesting Scotland experts, covering the tree species commonly found in Scotland. From seed provenance, tree diseases and propagation to history and lore, this single source contains all the information you need to select the right trees for your site and grow them successfully. An invaluable reference for anyone with an interest in our trees and woodlands.

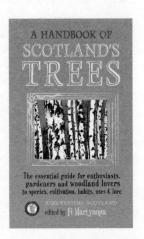

"It's the book I've always wanted, and it's a delight."
RODDY FAIRLEY, SCOTTISH NATURAL HERITAGE
Fi Martynoga, ed. • £12.99 • Revised ed. ISBN: 9781908643827